# Black Pioneers
## *The Untold Stories of African Merchants*

By Phakamisa Ndzamela

ROCK
HOPPER
BOOKS

Rockhopper Books
Cape Town, South Africa

# CONTENTS

# Foreword

"People need to have a history of successes to believe that things can be done. Where people or communities have a history of failures, or of restricted progress and development, they come to believe that everything is impossible."
— Dr Sam Motsuenyane, founding Chairman of African Bank

For far too long, the roots of Black economic development have at best remained not widely told and therefore remain unknown and ignored; at worst lay buried deep beneath layers upon layers of misinformation, unjust legislation, and societal attitudes that predicated servitude over entrepreneurial ambition.

This prevailing ignorance of our own history means that the stories of pioneering Black entrepreneurs are in danger of being lost, precisely at the moment when they are most needed. As our nation grapples with serious economic challenges and the scourge of corruption in the public and private sectors, the role of black economic empowerment is being brought into question. These stories, however, bring renewed inspiration and optimism.

"The Untold Stories of Black South African Merchants Who Defied the Odds" is a celebration of the audacity of Black entrepreneurs. Their achievements are all the more remarkable when considering our history — and the determination of the racist National Party government to stymie Black economic participation on their own terms — as leaders of Black economic development. In their attempts to transcend their circumstances, and shedding the cloak of victimhood to write their own stories of success, they proved that the capacity to achieve the extraordinary exists within us all.

This is the powerful inheritance they have left to us. At African Bank, we regard ourselves as stewards of a rich heritage in which Black business people pooled their considerable talents to create an institution that would walk alongside the underserved on the path to prosperity.

African Bank was established to support the ambitions of Black entrepreneurs, and the stories of some of the remarkable people who played a pivotal role in the creation of our Bank, are to be found within these pages.

Despite having heard our founding story many times, I am still enthralled by the idea that African Bank was started with just R70! That, to me, is the epitome of audacity. That invaluable quality is the golden thread that weaves its way through this collection of stories. Audacity is the secret ingredient that empowers seemingly ordinary people to create something greater than themselves. The legacy of these audacious pioneers can be seen in virtually every township where, despite the circumstances, the entrepreneurial spirit still thrives. Through this book, we hope to preserve the memory of those business leaders who led by example, and uplifted those around them as they ascended the business ladder. Better still, we hope these stories will inspire a new generation of Black business leaders to emerge and take their place in the long line of extraordinary leaders, who drive Black economic development as an essential and critical ingredient for a prosperous future of our beautiful country, and, dare I say, the African continent as a whole.

Once such business leader was Dr Sam Motsuenyane, who sadly passed away this year. Dr Motsuenyane was, and remains, an inspiration to us all. He was an astute businessman, a man of integrity, and a passionate advocate for Black economic empowerment. We are honoured to be able to follow in his footsteps, walking alongside our people on the path to prosperity. The greatest tribute we could pay to him is to be audacious in our pursuit of his vision — an African bank for the people, by the people, serving the people.

We hope that the stories told in this book will not only inspire readers but spark important conversations as we grapple with the present realities. May these stories serve as beacons of hope and catalysts for positive change. Together, let us celebrate the audacious spirit of African Bank and the enduring legacy of Black business excellence.

**Thabo Dloti**
**African Bank Chairman of the Board**

# INTRO

In the annals of South Africa's rich and diverse history, the narratives of black merchants who defiantly carved out spaces of enterprise amidst the tumultuous backdrop of apartheid and its cascading socio-political constraints, stand as beacons of resilience and innovation.

**The Untold Stories of Black South African Merchants Who Defied the Odds** aims to shed light on this vital chapter of South African history, by threading together the entrepreneurial journeys of select individuals and institutions, illustrating how they transcended the period's adversities to etch their names into the tapestry of the country's economic legacy.

From the vision-driven enterprise of African Bank to the indomitable spirit of women like Constance Ntshona, Epainette Mbeki and Sally Motlana, this collection of stories captures the essence of determination and foresight. The entrepreneurial ventures of individuals like SJJ Lesolang, AN Gadi and HM Pitje, not only signify personal triumph, but

also reflect the broader Black Consciousness of Business; a movement underlining the nexus of entrepreneurship and identity politics. Moreover, these stories shed some light on the ramifications of pivotal events and policies, such as the Group Areas Act and the 1976 riots, on the black business community, highlighting the intricate interplay of history, business, and individual agency.

A portion of this book focuses on and pays homage to the resilient women of the era. The apartheid system, deeply rooted in patriarchy, posed even more compounded challenges for black women. They grappled not only with racial discrimination but also gender-based prejudices, making their journey in the business realm all the more arduous. Women had to manoeuvre through societal norms that often relegated them to secondary roles; restrictive laws that limited their economic activities, and a patriarchal business culture. Yet, in this adverse setting, they rose, establishing themselves in trade, retail, and more, making indelible marks on the country's economic history.

# DUCTION

While these case studies epitomise the spirit and challenges of that era, they are but a fraction of the countless narratives from this time — stories of unyielding men and women determined to redefine their destinies. These stories shed light on the resistance and ingenuity embedded in South Africa's economic history, and they are reflective of the fortitude of countless others whose stories remain untold.

Their inclusion in this compilation is based on the oral and rich archival material available, ensuring a robust and evidence-backed recounting of their exploits. Special attention was given to individuals and entities that showcased a diverse range of responses to apartheid's restrictions, from direct resistance and activism to strategic adaptations and innovations in business.

Rich in detail and varied in scope, these stories were sourced from historical archives, interviews, newspaper articles, and autobiographies. The aim was to include both men and women who played pivotal roles across different sectors and regions, thus painting a broader picture of black business

under apartheid. The resonance of these tales in contemporary South Africa cannot be overstated. In an age where the nation grapples with questions of identity, economic empowerment, and redressing historical inequities, these stories remind us of the foundation upon which the modern South African business landscape was built. They echo the timeless values of perseverance, ingenuity, and courage, serving as both inspiration and cautionary tales for future generations.

This book does more than recount history; it reveres the enduring spirit of black South African merchants — a spirit of unwavering defiance and exceptional innovation that, against all conceivable odds, thrived. As you delve into the pages that follow, may you not only find historical accounts, but also discern the undying spirit of a people, the soul of a nation, and the timeless lessons that history offers to those willing to listen.

# African Bank
## An enterprise created by African business people

*"We regard the African Bank as the greatest symbol of the black man's creative power in South Africa. Therefore, it is a monument that must not be allowed to die nor to remain small due to lack of support."*

— Sam Motsuenyane, NAFCOC Presidential Address, delivered in Mamelodi on January 23, 1979.[1]

Motsuenyane, S.M: An Address [Presidential] Delivered at Mamelodi, January 23, 1979

# THE ORIGINS OF AFRICAN BANK

The establishment of African Bank in 1975 was a testament to the resilience and determination of black South Africans who dared to embark on business ventures during the trying times of apartheid.

It was at the 1964 inaugural conference of the National African Federated Chamber of Commerce (NAFCOC) in the township of Orlando, Johannesburg, that the idea of an African bank was first mooted. A guest speaker at the conference, Collins Ramusi, had highlighted the importance and potential impact of black-controlled financial institutions.[2] A lawyer by training, Ramusi had just returned from the US after studying at Northwestern University. It was the same period that Sam Motsuenyane, the honorary life member of NAFCOC and co-founder of African Bank, had also just returned from the US after completing a BSc degree at the University of North Carolina.[3] Both men had brought home invaluable insights from their stints abroad.

During the conference, Ramusi shared his experiences from the US, where he had observed that black Americans had successfully started their financial services firms, such as banks; building societies, and insurance companies.[4] While black South Africans had historically sought mechanisms to bank and protect their money, it was arguably Ramusi who planted the transformative seed at the 1964 conference that would change the historical trajectory of financial services in South Africa.

Yet it took more than a visionary idea to create a tangible institution. Someone had to rile up the crowd to go beyond the exciting grand talk of a bank. The prime mover was the Mamelodi businessman, Hezekiah Mothibe Pitje, popularly known as HM Pitje.[5] Word is that Pitje put out a challenge by placing an initial sum of money on the table, challenging other delegates to follow suit and contribute to the formation of the bank. But that was not enough.[6]

Wits Historical Papers Research Archive, Skota Papers: WF Nkomo

Wits Historical Papers Research Archive, Skota Papers: Collins Ramusi

2   UNISA Archives, ACC290, A History of the Black Bank, Black Giant Awake, NAFCOC Magazine, 1974, p5
3   UNISA Archives, ACC290, Young, but daily growing, The African Bank: A Corporate Report Supplement to Financial Mail, 22 November 1985, pII
4   UNISA Archives, ACC290, A History of the Black Bank, Black Giant Awake, NAFCOC Magazine, 1974, p5
5   UNISA Archives, ACC290, Motsuenyane, S.M: An Address [Presidential] Delivered at Mamelodi, January 23, 1979
6   UNISA Archives, ACC290, A History of the Black Bank, Black Giant Awake, NAFCOC Magazine, 1974, p5

*"Unfortunately, I was not there, but he (Pitje) said he put R30 on the table, inspiring others to follow suit. He had a mini-bus and used it to travel across the provinces, trying to get people to join in the endeavour to start this African bank,"* recalled Vuyelwa Alice Pitje, HM Pitje's widow.[7]

## At the 1964 NAFCOC meeting, only R70 was raised to start African Bank.[8]

The journey ahead, however, was still fraught with challenges. It would take eleven years of capital raising, conferences and lobbying for the concept of an African bank to become a reality. Over the decade, the enthusiasm to start a bank inflated and deflated. The spark was kept alive by several people, including influential speakers at NAFCOC conferences. For example, Dr William Frederick Nkomo underscored the importance of self-reliance and unity, while Prince Mangosuthu Buthelezi would stress that black businessmen were not inferior to their white counterparts.[9] Nkomo was a highly respected leader and community activist who started a career as a teacher and then advanced to become a medical doctor.[10]

Buthelezi would later go on to found the Inkatha Freedom Party (IFP) and become the Chief Minister of the KwaZulu Bantustan.

7   Author's interview with Mrs Vuyelwa Alice Pitje, June 16, 2023
8   Motsoenyane, S, A Testament of Hope, p98
9   UNISA Archives, ACC290, A History of the Black Bank, Black Giant Awake, NAFCOC Magazine, 1974, p5-6
10  Ngole, N, Rand Daily Mail, Tributes will be paid to Dr William Nkomo, Saturday, July 30, 1977, p10

The turning point came when Motsuenyane, who had become NAFCOC President, led a delegation of business leaders to England in 1972, where they met with the management of global banking giant Barclays.

Motsuenyane, armed with compelling data, informed Barclays' leadership that while black South Africans deposited their savings in white-owned banks, they did not own a stake in these established financial institutions. He conveyed the intention of black South Africans to establish their own bank; a message that Barclays responded to positively, promising assistance in whatever form necessary. The support started with Barclays offering banking training to black people.[11]

While Barclays had committed to helping with the training of staff for African Bank, as well as capital provision, government approval was still needed. Motsuenyane knew of a World Bank annual general meeting taking place in Nairobi, Kenya, attended by Finance Ministers. He took advantage of the presence at the gathering of the then South African Finance Minister Dr Nico Diederichs. Black leaders opposed to apartheid walked out of the meeting room when Diederichs started addressing the meeting. However, Motsuenyane seized the opportunity during lunch to discuss with Diederichs the necessity of government approval for the formation of African Bank. Upon returning to South Africa, Diederichs facilitated Motsuenyane's request, and African Bank was granted permission to register. However, Barclays could not be the only shareholding bank in African Bank. Other South African major banks had to participate too.[12]

In his opening address to the NAFCOC African Bank Fundraising Conference in Mamelodi on September 7, 1974, Motsuenyane shared the following update:

*"We have so far raised three-fifths of the capital that we are expected to raise before the registration of our proposed black bank."*[13]

Motsuenyane had kept the speech short, remarking:

*"The black bank must become a reality, and I have no doubt that it will. This day is not a day for eloquent speeches; it is a day for action..."*[14]

[11] UNISA Archives, ACC290, Young but daily growing. *The African Bank, A Corporate Report Supplement to Financial Mail*, November 22, 1985, p4-12
Motsuenyane S, *A Testament of Hope, The Autobiography of Dr Sam Motsuenyane*, p606-608.
[13] UNISA Archives, ACC290, SM Motsuenyane, NAFCOC Opening Address, Mamelodi African Bank Fundraising Conference, September 7, 1974.
[14] Ibid.

National Archives of South Africa: RB, RB160
Old African Bank Logo

# The **Structuring** of **African Bank**

As the path cleared for the bank's inception, a debate ensued on what the appropriate name of the new bank would be. Several proposals were considered, including African National Bank of SA, the First African National Bank, the United African Bank, and the Black Bank of SA.[15] Ultimately the name that won the day was: *"The African Bank of South Africa Limited"*.

On July 30, 1975, the Registrar of Banks issued a letter affirming that approval had been granted for the establishment of the bank's head office on the 6th Floor of the Northern Trust Building, 30 Loveday Street, Johannesburg. However, this was subject to approval by the Department of Bantu Administration and Development.[16] The following day on July 31, 1975, The African Bank of South Africa Limited ("African Bank") was formally incorporated under the registration number 75/2526.[17]

With the entity now officially named The African Bank of South Africa Limited, the next step was to design a fitting logo to build the brand's identity. The chosen logo was a tree with a sturdy brown stem. Above the stem, the tree's thick arms — the branches — stretched out, bearing the words in green "The African Bank of South Africa Limited". The way the text was arranged above the stem evoked the image of branches adorned with green leaves. The tree provided protection and shelter, reflecting the bank's commitment to safeguard and protect depositors' funds. Furthermore, as trees bear fruit, seeds, and wood, the logo also embodied the bank's promise of yielding benefits in the form of interest and security.[18]

Despite the capital raising, a lot of other heavy lifting was required to get the bank started. This included securing premises, obtaining safety equipment, electronic machinery, interviewing and recruiting the right staff; preparing handbooks of instruction and engaging with government. As the bank's deposits were to be entrusted to people, it was crucial to create the right conditions and benefits for employees, including medical and pension benefits. African employees were to undergo training in the shareholder white banks. The bank's management insisted that *"men and women will receive equal treatment"*.[19]

[15] UNISA Archives, ACC290.NAFCOC Minutes of the Ninth Annual Conference, Held at Mafikeng, From May 17-20, 1973, p6
[16] NATIONAL ARCHIVES OF SOUTH AFRICA, RB, RB508/6, Letter from the Registrar of Bank W Louw to A.E. Wentzel, The African Bank of South Africa Limited (Proposed Banking Institution, 5 August 1977)
[17] NATIONAL ARCHIVES OF SOUTH AFRICA, RB, RB160, African Bank of South Africa Limited, Prospectus, August 29, 1973, p7.
[18] UNISA Archives, ACC290, The African Bank South Africa Limited, The Present Position by Wentzel A.E, General Manager-Designate, p2.
[19] Ibid

In November 1975, African Bank was granted provisional registration to operate as a bank. However, it could neither accept deposits nor advance loans until an auditor's certificate demonstrated that the bank's paid-up capital had reached R1m.

The authorities also approved the use of *"Afribank"* as an abbreviation of the name African Bank.[20]

The first branch of African Bank was located at Stand 700, Hebron Road, Zone 16, Ga-Rankuwa, Bophuthatswana, with a second branch earmarked for Soweto.[21] On November 22, 1975, African Bank hosted a grand celebration in Ga-Rankuwa, with esteemed guests including representatives from the Registrar of Financial Institutions, Wynand Louw and his wife.[22]

Word is that in the festivities leading up to the opening of the first branch in Ga-Rankuwa on December 1, 1975, eight cattle and about 20 sheep were slaughtered. As the celebrations drew to a close, heavy rain began to fall. In several African cultures, this is considered a blessing, and on that occasion it prompted the joyful crowd to exclaim, *'Pula, pula'* amid the downpour.[23]

But who were these audacious black business people, who took upon themselves the task of steering the establishment of African Bank? On its board of directors were the merchants Amos Nzimeni Gadi, a general dealer from Lusikisiki in the Transkei; Patrick Goodwyn Gumede, a general dealer from Madadeni Township, Newcastle, Natal; Solomon Joel Jack Lesolang, a garage proprietor from Zone 4 Ga-Rankuwa; Registone Roy Mbongwe, a general dealer from Adams Mission in Natal; Motsuenyane, an agronomist; John Henry Khaas, a beer hall owner from Mahwelereng, Potgietersrus; and Enos Zwelabantu Sikakane, a Minister of Religion from Plessislaer, Edendale, Natal. The board also included white bankers as directors and these were Henry Sargent Liebenberg, Desmond Havinga and Colin Harry Waterson, all from Johannesburg. The first

General Manager of the bank was Allan Edward Wentzel, a chartered accountant and banker.[24]

On the origins of African Bank, Wentzel shared that he met Motsuenyane through the South African Council of Churches (SACC). The SACC had worked with NAFCOC ahead of the registration of the bank. Wentzel recalled that the SACC had raised funds from German churches for administration work and publicity purposes leading up to the registration of African Bank. Wentzel credited Motsuenyane for bringing in a group of very intelligent black directors. "We were able to take people with very limited financial skills in banking to become part of the Board of Directors; to form a strong Board of Directors and that was under the gentle guidance of Dr Motsuenyane," recalled Wentzel. He would add that at the time there were not many black directors in South Africa who had served as seniors at a bank.

A call was made that 49 percent of the total issued shares of African Bank would be held by African private investors, 30 percent by white financial institutions and 21 percent by the African *"homeland"* governments.[25] The final handwritten prospectus showed that initially, the authorised capital of African Bank was set at R1m, divided into 1m shares at R1 per share. However, through a special resolution dated August 13, 1975, the authorised share capital was increased to R1.3m, divided into 1.3m shares at R1 per share.[26]

In the early stages of its operation, it was anticipated that African Bank would receive support and guidance from five shareholder banks, well-versed in banking and familiar with the business affairs of black people. It was agreed that the shareholder banks would apply for 300 000 ordinary shares at R1 per share.[27]

The five primary banks holding shares in African Bank were Barclays National Bank Limited, The Standard Bank of South Africa Limited, Nedbank Limited, Die Trust Bank van Afrika Beperk and Volkskas Beperk.[28]

[19] NATIONAL ARCHIVES OF SOUTH AFRICA (19), RB160, RB, Application for Registration as a General Bank, 7 November 1975
[20] UNISA Archives, ACC290, The African Bank South African Limited, The Present Position by Wentzel A.E., General Manager
[21] NATIONAL ARCHIVES OF SOUTH AFRICA (15), RB160, Letter by NAFCOC President SM Motsuenyane to W Louw, Registrar of Financial Institutions, December 17, 1975
[22] UNISA Archives, ACC290, Voting list daily growing, The African Bank: A Corporate Report Supplement to Financial Mail November 22, 1985, p14
[23] NATIONAL ARCHIVES OF SOUTH AFRICA, RB, RB160, African Bank of South African Limited, Prospectus August 29, 1975, p6
[24] UNISA Archives ACC290, African Bank Progress
[25] NATIONAL ARCHIVES OF SOUTH AFRICA, RB, RB160, African Bank of South African Limited, Prospectus (handwritten in blue ink), August 29, 1975, p1
[26] NATIONAL ARCHIVES OF SOUTH AFRICA, RB, RB160, African Bank of South Africa Limited, Prospectus August 29, 1975, p12
[27] NATIONAL ARCHIVES OF SOUTH AFRICA, RB, RB160 SR, Relationship between the Bank and its Shareholding Banks, Letter from A.E. Wentzel to The Registrar of Banks, April 28, 1977, p1

...the number of directors shall not be less than eight nor mor...
than ten, of whom not more than three nor less than two sh...
be directors appointed by the shareholding Banks.

160/5

Aandeelhouding soos op 14 November 1975.

| | capital | % |
|---|---|---|
| Shareholding Banks (each holding 60 000 shares) | 300 000 | 30 |
| Mr. V. Leeuw | 16 480 | 1,6 |
| Mr. N.G. Moja | 14 000 | 1,4 |
| Mr. A.J. Shadi | 21 903 | 2,2 |
| Mr. S.M. Motsuenyane | 15 300 | 1,5 |
| SA Technology Development Group (Pty) Ltd | 90 000 | 9,0 |
| | 457 683 | 45,768 |
| Other shareholders (less than 1%) | 742 317 | |
| | 1 200 000 | |

Aandeelhouding soos op 3 Januarie 1979:

| | number | % |
|---|---|---|
| a) Shareholding Banks | 300 000 | 24,0 |
| b) i) Gazankulu Government Service | 25 000 | 2,0 |
| ii) Kwa-Zulu Government Service | 25 000 | 2,0 |
| c) i) Mr. V.T. Leeuw | 16 480 | 1,3 |
| ii) Mr. N.G. Moja | 14 000 | 1,1 |
| iii) Mr. S.M. Motsuenyane | 15 300 | 1,2 |
| iv) Mr. A.J. Shadi | 24 053 | 1,9 |
| d) S.A. Technology Development Group | 37 588 | 3,1 |
| e) Other shareholders (1 546) | 457 421 | 36,6 |
| | 792 579 | 63,4 |
| | 1 250 000 | 100,0 |

In May 1975, directors of African Bank noted as shareholders were Amos Nzimeni Gadi, Registone Roy Mbongwe and Collins Molapateni Ramusi, each linked to 100 shares.[29] It is not clear if this was the exact total of shares that the above-mentioned parties each owned.

As of November 14, 1975, the shareholding banks owned 300 000 shares or 25 percent of African Bank. Motsuenyane owned a 1.3 percent stake or 15 300 shares and Mr NG Moja held 14 000 shares or 1.2 percent. Other black individuals commanded larger shares and these included Mr AJ Shadi with 21 903 shares or 1.8 percent and Mr V Leeuw 16 480 or 1.4 percent. The majority of the shares or 742 317 (about 61.85 percent), were linked to other shareholders who individually owned less than 1 percent. A company called SA Technology Development Group (Pty) Ltd held 90 000 shares or 7.5 percent.[30]

When the shareholder relationship between the white-controlled shareholder banks and African Bank was established, it was envisaged that the former would assist the latter in creating accounting systems. In addition, the white-controlled banks agreed to second a total of eight staff members to African Bank for a period of five years.[31]

[29] NATIONAL ARCHIVES OF SOUTH AFRICA, RB, RB60, Particulars of Subscriber, May 30, 1975
[30] NATIONAL ARCHIVES OF SOUTH AFRICA, RB, 1(3)(60, African Bank of South Africa Limited, Prospectus (handwritten in blue ink), August 29, 1975, p1
[31] Ibid, p2

# RESTRICTIONS ON AFRICAN BANK:

## A LETTER FROM
## HENDRIK VERWOERD BUILDING

A condition for establishing African Bank was that it would open parallel branches, where practical. This meant for every branch opened in the black-occupied urban areas, another branch would be opened in the homelands. Competition between African Bank and the white-owned shareholding banks was to be expected in the normal course of doing business.[32] However, African Bank was unjustly prohibited from operating branches in places classified as *"white areas"*.

On February 18, 1976, Wentzel, the General Manager of African Bank, wrote to Wynand Louw at the Registrar of Banks, Department of Finance, requesting permission to open branches in white areas. The idea was to open a branch of African Bank in white areas with a high concentration of black workers. This would have been in places such as bus termini, railway stations and so forth.

The objective was to offer convenient banking facilities to Africans and minimise the risks associated with carrying money between their centres of work and areas of residence,[33] significantly reducing the risk of robbery.[35]

*"It is felt that this service would not only provide good business for this Bank but would also provide a public service in helping to eliminate the many robberies (and worse) which take place at present, for example, between Park Station and Soweto; we are sure that the South African Police would support us in this,"* Wentzel argued.[34]

Ibid
NATIONAL ARCHIVES OF SOUTH AFRICA. JIS 1139/4 Deposit/registration Letter from A.F. Wentzel to W. Louw, Registrar of Banks, Department of Finance, February 18, 1976.
Ibid
NATIONAL ARCHIVES OF SOUTH AFRICA. BTS R18/60 Die Minister. The African Bank of South African Limited: Stigting Van Takkantore in Blanke Gebiede Met 'n Hoe Samedromming Van Bantoe-werkers, May 14, 1976.

National Archives of South Africa: RB, RB160
Letters to AE Wentzel

National Archives of South Africa: RB, RB160
Letters to AE Wentzel

Louw subsequently wrote to the Minister of Finance seeking approval to establish the bank in white areas. Although not confirmed, it seemed there had been a verbal engagement between Louw and the Finance Minister prior to the letter.

The letter written by Louw in Afrikaans has since been translated into English, and reads in part:

*"During an oral discussion on the matter, you indicated that you wanted to discuss it with the Minister of Bantu Administration and Development. This Office is of the opinion that the request to open branches in special places in white areas has merit."*[36]

A month later, a letter from the private secretary of the Ministry of Finance, at Hendrik Verwoerd Building in Cape Town, and addressed to the Registrar of Financial Institutions, tersely advised in less than 50 words that the Cabinet would not, at that stage, approve the request to open a branch in a white area.[37]

Louw, as the bearer of the disappointing news, wrote to African Bank as follows:

*"I write with further reference to your letter dated 18 February 1976 and wish to advise that the Government does not see its way clear, at this stage, to accede to your request to establish branches in White areas with a high density of Bantu workers."*[38]

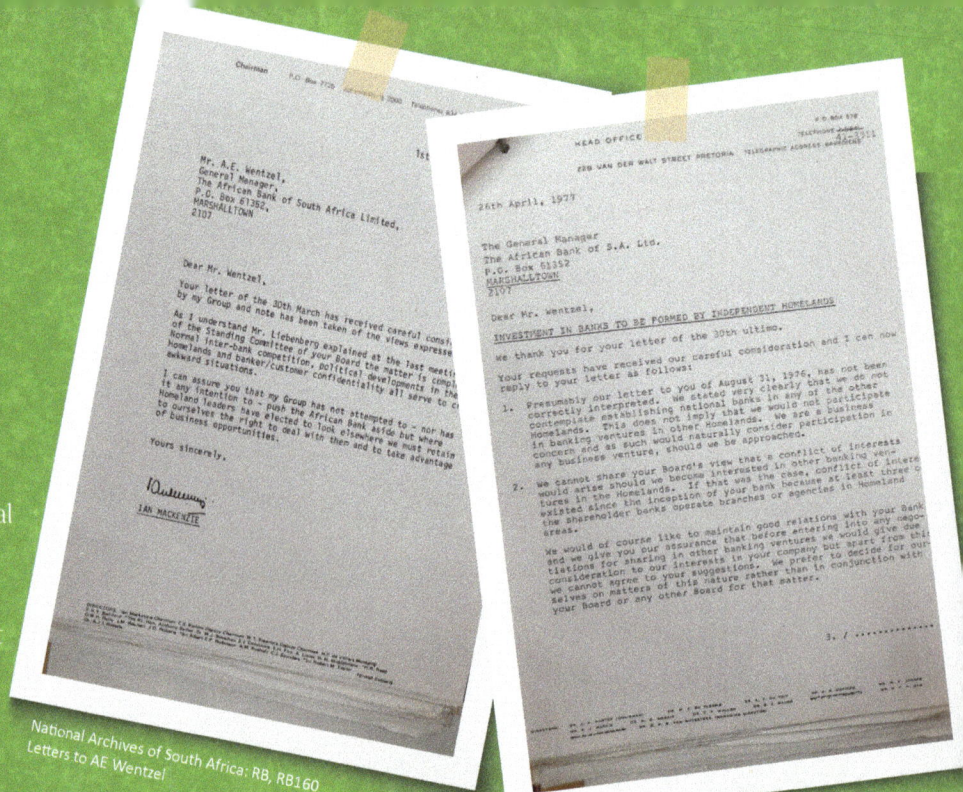

36 Ibid
   NATIONAL ARCHIVES OF SOUTH AFRICA, RB, RB160, Die Registrateur van Finansiële Instellings, The African Bank of
   South Africa Limited, Stigting Van Takkantore in Blanke Gebiede Met 'n Hoë Samedromming Van Bantoewerkers, June 4, 1976.
   NATIONAL ARCHIVES OF SOUTH AFRICA, RB, RB160, Letter from the Registrar of Banks JW Louw to The General Manager
   African Bank of South Africa Limited, 17-6-1976.

However, African Bank was undeterred and devised a new strategy. Wentzel again wrote to the Registrar of Banks; this time proposing the establishment of an *"agency"* rather than a branch. The agency was envisioned as an office with no books of account and limited cash kept overnight. All permanent records would be maintained in the parent branch at Ga-Rankuwa, and surplus cash would be deposited to a convenient commercial bank. The staff required to operate the agency would come from the Ga-Rankuwa branch on the days required and no permanent officers would be attached to the proposed office. The agency would simply receive deposits and pay out withdrawals. Other services would be coordinated for the convenience of customers through the Ga-Rankuwa branch, with operations expected to be weekly. The plea to open an agency on the corner of Bloed and Bosman Streets, Pretoria, aimed to provide banking services to the African bus and train commuters passing through the area, so that they did not carry pay cheques and cash with them during travels. This would help with reducing risk of loss and theft.[39]

On August 5, 1976, Wentzel visited the Registrar to discuss recent developments at African Bank, including the proposed agency. The expectation was that the agency would conduct its business from a rented office, so the issue of African Bank acquiring a fixed property in a white area did not arise.[40]

A year after the initial application, on February 8, 1977, Louw would write that the establishment of the agency by the Ga-Rankuwa branch of African Bank at the corner of Bloed and Bosman Streets, Pretoria, had finally been approved.[41]

# The shareholding banks and 'ethnic bank' problems

As the political landscape shifted in 1976, the homeland governments were being offered **"independence"**. This change meant the creation of new republics known as Bantustans, each with its own institutions, including banks. This geopolitical development had significant implications for African Bank. The bank had hoped that with the development of independent homelands, it would be well-placed to serve as a convenient banking facility for financial transactions between black populations in South Africa and those in the homelands.[42]

However, what African Bank had not anticipated was the shareholding banks establishing exclusive relationships with other black groups, particularly homeland governments, resulting in direct competition with it. African Bank would later discover that once the independent homelands were established in 1976, Volkskas would enter into agreements to start a bank with the homeland government of the Transkei Republic.[43] The directors of African Bank expressed dissatisfaction over such arrangements without prior consultation.

39  NATIONAL ARCHIVES OF SOUTH AFRICA, RB, RB160, Establishment of An Agency in Pretoria, Letter from A.F. Wentzel to W. Louw, Registrar of Banks, August 6, 1976
40  NATIONAL ARCHIVES OF SOUTH AFRICA, RB, RB160, Notes of a meeting between Wentzel and The Registrar of Banks, August 9, 1976
41  NATIONAL ARCHIVES OF SOUTH AFRICA, RB, RB160, Letter from W. Louw to A.F. Wentzel, Establishment of an Agency in Pretoria, February 8, 1977
42  NATIONAL ARCHIVES OF SOUTH AFRICA, RB, RB160, African Bank of South Africa Limited, Prospectus, August 29, 1975, p4
43  Ibid

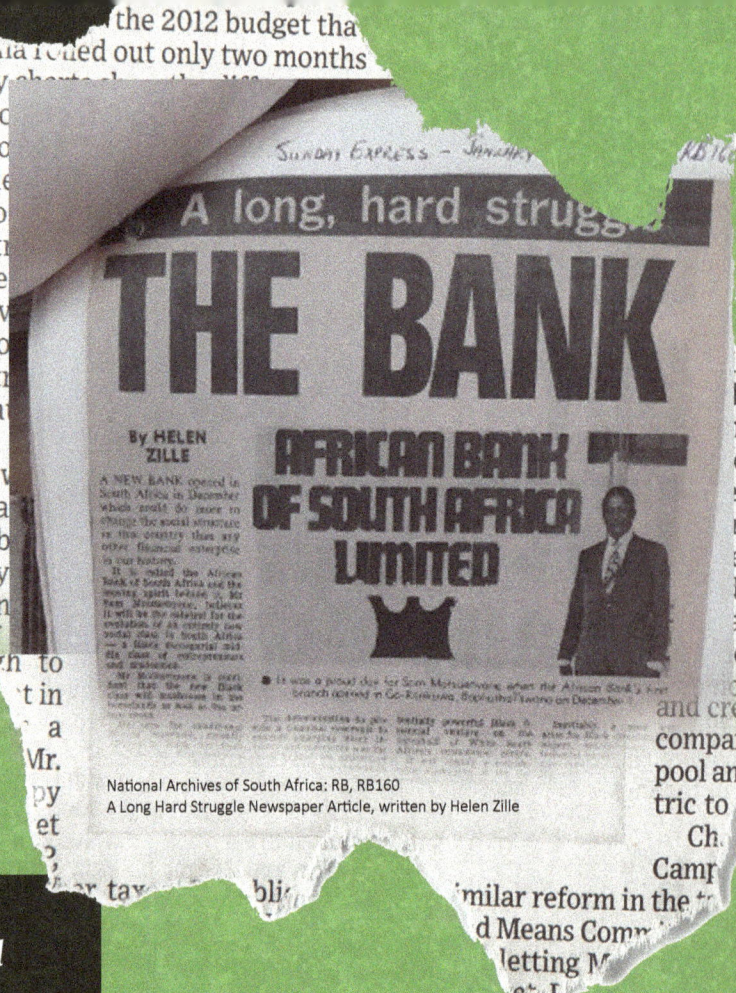

National Archives of South Africa: RB, RB160
A Long Hard Struggle Newspaper Article, written by Helen Zille

" There was an unhappiness in the Board of this Bank [The African Bank of South Africa Limited] at that stage that such an arrangement should have been entered into without consultation with the Board of this Bank. We have recently learnt that as far back as 1969, when Volkskas Beperk opened its branch in Umtata, it had promised the homeland Government of the time that after independence it would be prepared to enter into the arrangement, which had subsequently resulted in the formation of the Bank of Transkei Ltd. In mid-1976, it was learnt that Bophuthatswana would be moving towards independence and also desired to form a separate bank in that homeland."[44]

The directors of African Bank were uneasy about the controlling interest of Volkskas in The Bank of Transkei. Especially concerning was the news that with the granting of *"independence"* to homeland governments in 1976, The Bank of Transkei planned to expand its branch network in that homeland. This would lead to competition with African Bank.[45]

The concern of the directors of African Bank was not unfounded. In June 1976, a headline in the *Rand Daily Mail* proclaimed that *"Volkskas holds reins in new Transkei bank"*. Volkskas was reported as the controlling shareholder, providing management skills and making its Umtata building the new headquarters of The Bank of Transkei.[46]

44  Ibid
45  Ibid, p3
46  Own Correspondent, Rand Daily Mail, Friday, June 25, 1976

To complicate matters further, it emerged that the Bophuthatswana homeland had also engaged with Volkskas to establish a national bank. Although Volkskas apparently did not encourage the Bophuthatswana leadership in their endeavour, Volkskas had been asked to open additional branches in Bophuthatswana. This prompted the black directors of African Bank to write to all the shareholding banks questioning their involvement in what was termed *"ethnic banks"*.[47]

Essentially, the board of African Bank believed that it was unfair for the shareholding banks to participate in their bank and the competing ethnic banks at the same time. The black board of directors proposed restrictions on shareholder banks' involvement in African Bank, suggesting that Volkskas should be barred from appointing directors to the Board and Standing Committee. However, they also realised that if other banks operated like Volkskas, it could lead to a complete lack of representation from shareholding banks on the Board and Standing Committee.

The end goal of African Bank was to be completely black-controlled, but it seemed premature to effect an abrupt end to the shareholding relationship. To resolve the challenge, several options were considered, including forcing conflicted banks to be excluded from African Bank management but continue to hold shares and/or sell their shares to unconflicted banks. The other alternative was for the conflicted shareholding banks to sell their shares to African investors.[48]

However, the Registrar of Banks disagreed, stressing the need for African Bank to continue receiving technical assistance from the five white shareholding banks and that these banks ought to have been restrained from working with the Bantu homelands due to their shareholding in African Bank. Instead, the Registrar of Banks found it necessary for African Bank to still get technical assistance from white banks and not disturb the relations it had with them.[49] Volkskas, on the other hand, was clear in its stance, stating that while it did not contemplate to establish national banks in the homelands, this did not imply it would not participate in banking ventures in the homelands.[50]

> *"We are a business concern and as such would naturally consider participation in any business venture, should we be approached,"* it stated.[51]

Volkskas did not see the conflict of interest in pursuing other banking ventures in the homelands, making the point that at least three of the shareholder banks already operated branches or agencies there. Volkskas' only assurance to African Bank was that it would consider its interests in African Bank before embarking on any new venture.[52]

> *"Should our attitude be unacceptable to your Board, we would like to be prepared to withdraw our representation from your Board and from the Standing Committee, provided that suitable arrangement can be made for our shareholding to be taken over,"* Volkskas remarked.[53]

47 NATIONAL ARCHIVES OF SOUTH AFRICA, HB, BB60 Relationship Between the Bank and its Shareholding Banks, Letter from A.F. Wentzel to The Registrar of Banks, April 28, 1977, p3-4
48 Ibid
49 NATIONAL ARCHIVES OF SOUTH AFRICA, HB, BB60 Relationship Between The African Bank of South Africa Limited and its Shareholding Banks, Letter from Registrar of Banks W. Louw to the General Manager of The African Bank of South Africa Limited, May 25, 1977
50 NATIONAL ARCHIVES OF SOUTH AFRICA, HB, BB60 Participation in independent Banks to be formed by independent Homelands Letter from F.H. Venter, Assistant General Manager Volkskas to The General Manager, The African Bank of S.A. Ltd, April 26, 1977
51 Ibid
52 Ibid
53 Ibid

Barclays Bank adopted a friendlier tone, promising to consult with African Bank if investment opportunities arose in independent homelands.[54] Nedbank's view, on the other hand, was that while competition in urban areas could not be excluded between it and African Bank, it felt that Nedbank *"should not compete directly with the African Bank in typically African homelands or independent countries resulting from such homelands"*.[55]

Standard Bank was also cordial in its position, but in a manner that focused on its commercial interests. Ian Mackenzie of Standard Bank advised that the matter was complex, and the normal interbank competition and political developments in the homelands, coupled with banker-customer confidentiality created *"awkward situations"*. Mackenzie would add that his institution had made no attempt, nor intended to, sideline African Bank. However, if homeland leaders made a choice, then Standard Bank would reserve its right to deal with them and take advantage of the business opportunities.[56]

Thus, the granting of independence to homeland governments in 1976, and the resultant formation of new republics or Bantustans, presented African Bank with both opportunities and challenges. The bank hoped to leverage these geopolitical changes by offering financial services to the black population within these homelands. However, the involvement of shareholding banks, particularly Volkskas, in forming exclusive relationships with homeland governments to establish ethnic banks, resulted in unexpected competition.

This situation prompted considerable debate and tension between African Bank and its shareholding banks. African Bank's board deemed it unfair for these banks to participate in both their own operations and the ethnic banks, and even suggested imposing restrictions on their involvement in the bank's management. Yet, these suggestions were met with resistance from both the shareholding banks and the Registrar of Banks, who underscored the necessity of technical assistance from white banks.

# EXPANDING OPERATIONS AND PRODUCT LINE

From its early days, there was always an intention to grow African Bank through organic expansion and acquisitions, and into other areas of financial services. One of these identified areas of growth included offering business banking services to black business people and insurance brokerage services.

The bank's Ga-Rankuwa branch began receiving enquiries from business people seeking a more business-orientated service level. Consequently, the bank's leadership then proposed the introduction of an Afribank Business Account product, which required a minimum balance of R250 and capped at R15 000 for savings. A unique feature of this account was a *"no ledger fee"* provision. The balance of account attracted an interest of 3.5 percent per annum.[57] The Registrar of Banks did not object to the Afribank Business Account, as long as it complied with the Banks Act.[58]

[54] NATIONAL ARCHIVES OF SOUTH AFRICA, Banks to be formed by independent Homelands, Letter J.N. Abrahamsen, Nedbank Senior General Manager to The Directors, The African Bank of South Africa Limited, April 12, 1977
[55] NATIONAL ARCHIVES OF SOUTH AFRICA, Banks, Letter from Ian Mackenzie, Standard Bank Investment Corporation to A.F. Wentzel, General Manager, The African Bank of South Africa Limited, April 1, 1977
[56] NATIONAL ARCHIVES OF SOUTH AFRICA, Banks, Notes on AFRIBANK BUSINESS DEPOSIT ACCOUNTS
[57] NATIONAL ARCHIVES OF SOUTH AFRICA, Banks, AFRIBANK BUSINESS DEPOSIT ACCOUNTS, Letter from Registrar of Banks, W. Garrett to The General Manager of The African Bank of South Africa, January 27, 1978

African Bank had also started an insurance broking firm in collaboration with Glanvill Enthoven (SA) (Pty) Ltd. The partnership, known as Afribank Insurance Brokers (Pty) Ltd, had African Bank of South Africa owning 70 percent, with the remaining 30 percent held by Glanvill Enthoven (SA) (Pty) Ltd. African Bank later intended to acquire the 30 percent of the shares it did not own in Glanvill Enthoven; a move which was not opposed by the Registrar of Banks.[60]

Within five months of opening the first branch in Ga-Rankuwa, African Bank started negotiations with the Bantu Investment Corporation to acquire its savings bank division. Finalising the deal was subject to approval by the Transkei Government service and confirmation from the established homeland government that it was not interested in taking over.[61] The Bantu Investment Corporation was started by the apartheid regime as a racially segregating instrument aimed at funding black business people in the homelands.[62]

In the 11 months to end October 31, 1976, African Bank reported a loss of R130 436, partially due to shares issue expenses amounting to R64 917. In the year to end October 31, 1977, the loss had widened to R190 116. This loss included the R25 000 cost of goodwill paid to the Corporation for Economic Development Limited for the acquisition of a branch in Umtata. However, as of January 31, 1978, the bank reached a break-even point, indicating that its substantial development costs were now behind it. The bank's liabilities (deposits) had increased to R5m by January 31, 1978.[63]

# CONCLUSION

The formation of African Bank in 1975, the first **"black-controlled"** bank catering to black South Africans during the height of apartheid, represents an inspiring tale of resilience, innovation, and self-determination. Its birth amidst the harsh constraints of apartheid, offered a beacon of financial inclusion and empowerment to black South Africans, who had been systematically excluded from traditional financial systems.

The nascent stages of the bank were fraught with manifold challenges. Restrictive apartheid laws and the anticompetitive behaviour of established white-owned banks posed significant hurdles. However, despite these challenges, the founders persevered, fuelled by the vision of providing the black community with economic autonomy.

The bank also brought forth unforeseen opportunities. Its founders had envisioned it to fill a significant gap in the market and to spur economic activity on within the black community, thereby contributing to their financial upliftment. Close to five decades after its creation, African Bank continues to operate, despite having gone through different owners.

The story of African Bank is a testament to the desire for financial liberation in the face of institutionalised racism and serves as a remarkable chapter in South Africa's journey towards economic equity. Its legacy continues to underscore the critical importance of financial inclusivity in fostering social and economic justice.

59  NATIONAL ARCHIVES OF SOUTH AFRICA, RB160, Memorandum, The African Bank of S.A. Ltd. And Glanvill Enthoven (S.A) (Pty) Ltd.
60  NATIONAL ARCHIVES OF SOUTH AFRICA, RB160, Afribank Insurance Brokers buy-out, Letter from W Louw to The General manager, The African Bank Limited of South Africa, August 30, 1979
61  NATIONAL ARCHIVES OF SOUTH AFRICA, RB160 BIR Spearbanke in Die Transkei, May 28, 1976
62  Ndzamela, P. Native Merchants. The Building of the Black Business Class, p243
63  NATIONAL ARCHIVES OF SOUTH AFRICA, RB160, Progress of this Bank, Note from A.F Wentzel to the Registrar of Banks, Financial Institutions Office, March 21, 1978, p1-3

# Constance Ntshona

## A woman who defied apartheid and defined business excellence

Throughout history, black South African women have always stood as central figures in business, not merely as sidekicks or shop assistants in enterprises started by their husbands. Constance Khuziwe Blanche Ntshona (née Malunga) is one such remarkable woman. Born on November 19, 1925, in Kimberley, Ntshona was a trained nurse, but later became a trader. In the 1960s and 1970s, Ntshona ran a business called People's Suppliers in Soweto.[1]

Ntshona family archives:
Constance Ntshona

*"It was amazing the success that my mother got from that business. I cannot give you the profit and loss statements she had as it has been many years. But one thing that strikes me now when I look back; she supported two children outside the country and not at a very cheap rate either. If that can be used as a yardstick, so be it...," recalled Ntshona's son, Luvuyo Peter Ntshona.*

[1] National Archives of South Africa, BAO Vol No 3783, C100/6/3160, Application for South African Passport, Mrs Constance Khuziwe Ntshona, June 8, 1973

*"Whatever school I went to in Britain, more expensive than this side of the shores; I went there. My sister went to Waterford. Waterford was one of the best schools for the new up-and-coming community. We had a home in Dube Village. It was beautiful, I dare say. It was designed by my father. My mother maintained such a home and maintained the education of two growing children. I think this speaks well of the success she was achieving in People's Suppliers."[2]*

---

A *New York Times* article in April 1970, described Constance Ntshona as a prosperous businesswoman with a weekly turnover of R2 000.[3] A significant portion of those earnings went towards her children's education. The children began their schooling at a boarding school in Leribe, Lesotho, after which they then attended a school in the country's capital, Maseru. Subsequently, Nokuzola *"Zola"* Ntshona, the eldest of the two children, attended St Theresa's, a boarding school in Manzini, Swaziland. She spent five years there and excelled. Later, she enrolled for two years at the prestigious Waterford Kamhlaba School, a multi-racial school in Swaziland where prominent South African families also sent their children for better education. Some of the prominent surnames from South Africa during Nokuzola's time at Waterford included Guma and Gcabashe.[4]

Meanwhile, Luvuyo went to Nigeria to join his exiled father, Victor Scrape Ntshona, sometime between 1964 and 1965. The Ntshonas were determined to provide their children an education outside of the dumbed-down Bantu education system in South Africa.[5]

2    Author's interview with Luvuyo Peter Ntshona, June 14, 2023
3    New York Times, Black Elite in South Africa is well off but resentful, April 7, 1970, https://www.nytimes.com/1970/08/07/archives/black-elite-in-south-africa-is-well-off-but-resentful.html
4    Author's interview with Dr Nokuzola Ntshona, June 14, 2023
5    Author's interview with Luvuyo Peter Ntshona, June 14, 2023

Recalling the invaluable educational opportunities her mother provided her and Luvuyo, Dr Nokuzola Ntshona stated:

*"It was expensive. The school fees alone was R600 per year and the uniform was R200 for the blazer, tie, hat and skirt. It was an expensive school, but my mother managed to have me there, after which I went to the London University at Bedford College. She paid for that as well from the business."*[6]

---

When Dr Nokuzola Ntshona went to study abroad in 1971, the *Rand Daily Mail* ran an article about her decision to study biochemistry at Bedford in London and her aspirations to become a medical doctor.[7]

The Ntshona children fondly remember their days behind the counter at People's Suppliers serving customers, even though they were not involved in handling the cash.

*"Both of us actually spent a lot of time behind the counter, but not so much counting money. I vividly remember my mother meticulously counting the coins in her office, not notes. She was counting pennies most of the time. It was a laborious process,"* reminisced Luvuyo about his time in Soweto.

*"We were not involved in the counting of the money. We had to be outside and engage with the community. I recall how we used to package* **impuphu** *(maize meal). Back then, we did not have IWISA like we have today, which is already packaged. We had to portion out* **impuphu** *from a large bag based on customers' requirements."*[8]

6    Author's interview with Dr Nokuzola Ntshona, June 14, 2023
7    Rand Daily Mail, "Zola vows: I'll let no one down", Tuesday, August 10, 1971
8    Authors interview with Luvuyo Peter Ntshona, June 14, 2023

Luvuyo also remembered their many interactions with the community.

*"We often spent time in the community, and people would frequently visit. We'd share chips together. I was particularly fond of the fish and chips. However, my mother's **amagwinya** (fat cakes) were a bit too oily for my liking."*[9]

People's Suppliers wasn't just a store; it was a multifaceted business. It had a general store, a butchery, and a kitchen that sold mostly *amagwinya* and fish and chips. The business had a licence to open seven days a week, remembered Dr Nokuzola Ntshona.[10] According to several media reports, Ntshona also operated a dry-cleaning depot.[11]

Within the People's Suppliers complex, there was also a doctor who rented space for his clinic, reflecting the family's ethos of service. The general dealer was the primary attraction. The restaurant catered more to professionals like doctors and salespeople, serving them traditional dishes like *pap* or *samp* and meat.[12] The profits from People's Suppliers were not solely channelled towards the children's education. Luvuyo nostalgically spoke of the luxuries his mother indulged herself in. For instance, she drove a yellow Peugeot 404, a comfortable and highly regarded French car in those days. Later, Ntshona upgraded to an army-green Mercedes Benz 220 in the 1970s.[13]

*"She was doing pretty well for herself... The success of People's Suppliers was not just because of her character, resilience, singular focus or her desire to succeed and care for her family. The business also flourished because of her disciplined management and her deep connection with the community. Even now, when I visit Zola Mndeni, people recognise me, with some even moved to tears. I remember from my childhood, whenever we drove through Zola Mndeni, kids would excitedly shout 'Ntshona! Ntshona!' when we used to drive past."*[14]

# 'Ntshona! Ntshona!'

9 Ibid
10 Author's interview with Dr Nokuzola Ntshona, June 14, 2023
11 Staff Reporter, Rand Daily Mail, "Row brews over business award", March 13, 1973, p22
12 Author's interview with Luvuyo Peter Ntshona, June 14, 2023
13 Ibid
14 Ibid

**Luvuyo also noted that:**

*"She was in a league of her own, competing successfully with her male peers not just in business, but also in politics."[15]*

Politically, Ntshona was involved in the Urban Bantu Councils, which had been formed as part of the apartheid system of racial segregation to enable participation by urban Africans in their own administration.

---

*"My mother was a vicious, if you will; quite a staunch champion of showing that women can do it. Some of these organisations tended to be quite patriarchal."[16]*

Government records from March 1970 indicate that Ntshona applied for a passport to travel to Britain for a two- to three-month holiday. A letter addressed to the Bantu Affairs Commissioner, signed by GH Patten, the Senior Township's Superintendent, noted that Ntshona successfully operated a trading undertaking on stands 307 to 310 in Zola, Soweto. She was recognised as the owner of the house on site No. 1434 Pioneer Avenue, Dube Village, Soweto. Her financial accounts for amenities like rent, water and electricity were always settled on time.[17]
By April 1971, reports emerged that Ntshona

had travelled to Britain to study retail trends. During her absence, her daughter Zola and father, Mr Malunga, oversaw the business in Soweto. Self-funded, her tour to Europe included visits to major retailers such as Selfridges and Marks & Spencer; the fashionable Via Condotti Street in Rome, the Europa Centre in Berlin, the Spar Organisation headquarters in Holland, and several general dealers. Letters of introduction from her white business associates in Johannesburg facilitated her visits to these overseas business organisations. Ntshona's objective was to learn modern ways of running her business to compete better.[18]

*"We are competing with old established businesses in the city. To survive, we shall have to use effective modern business techniques to attract customers to our shops,"* Ntshona commented.

15   Ibid
16   Author's interview with Luvuyo Peter Ntshona, June 14, 2023
17   National Archives of South Africa, BAO Vol No 3783, C100/6/5160, Application for South African Passport, Mrs Constance Khuziwe Ntshona, March 9, 1970
18   Staff Reporter, Rand Daily Mail, "Woman on study tour", Thursday April 22, 1971, p5

She expressed dissatisfaction with how black people preferred to spend their incomes on business in the city instead of the townships, noting that:

*"I am not happy because a greater part of the earnings of Soweto people is spent in the city."*[19]

In the same year after the trip to Europe, Ntshona addressed the Johannesburg Chamber of Commerce on the challenges faced by black business people. As a member of NAFCOC, even during the height of apartheid, Ntshona courageously addressed the odds stacked against African traders. Speaking before a predominantly white audience at a Johannesburg Chamber of Commerce event, Ntshona declared:

*"The difficulties and frustrations of the African trader are a direct result of the same policies which divide our society into socially unequal sections, and which regrettably seem to receive wide acceptance from that section of society of which my audience is representative this afternoon."*[20]

Highlighting the deeper challenges, Ntshona spoke of how African traders started businesses without freehold rights to land, lacked access to bank overdraft facilities, and were excluded from state loans.

Bailey Archives: Constance Ntshona serving customers in her shop; Spar supplied goods to her shop

She pointed out that a number of African traders effectively "pawned" a substantial portion of their profits for years to wholesalers, who supplied them with goods at prices far more than those offered to certain chain stores. Without sufficient capital, these traders could not buy goods in bulk. As a result, African consumers shopped in urban areas to the disadvantage of African traders in the townships. Another challenge was that these traders were restricted to selling *"bread and butter"* items, which generated little profit. Ntshona also emphasised the socio-economic challenges in townships, which were plagued by poverty, oppression and rampant burglaries. Compounding this problem was the insurance industry's reluctance to cover African businesses.[21]

[19] Staff Reporter, Rand Daily Mail, "Woman on study tour", Thursday April 22, 1971, p3
[20] Sapa report in Rand Daily Mail, "Trade Reflects Black Poverty", Thursday, November 25, 1971, p4
[21] Sapa report in Rand Daily Mail, "Trade Reflects Black Poverty", Thursday, November 25, 1971, p4

Ntshona family archives: (Left) Young Dr Nokuzola Ntshona, Victor Scrape Ntshona (husband to Constance), Constance Ntshona and son Vuyo Ntshona

*"Notwithstanding all the hazards that we face as African traders; we are not asking for charity. We want to stand on our own feet,"* Ntshona said.[22]

Her son, Luvuyo, recalls that among the 13 or 14 employees at his mother's shop, there was also a night watchman or security guard. This was because she often travelled after 20h00, in the absence of a security van to handle cash transportation.[23]

Ntshona was known for being outspoken. At an annual general meeting of the South African Black Travellers Association in May 1972, she fervently advised salespeople against selling goods which put black people into unaffordable debt.

She warned that if the salesmen enticed the traders to buy more than they could sell, their funds would be tied in unsellable stock. In such an instance, Ntshona said, **"the salesman was morally responsible for the trader's bankruptcy"**.

During this meeting, Ntshona did not hold back, urging clothing manufacturers with no black salesmen to hire them, given that a significant portion of their revenue came from black customers.[24]

Ntshona's success was not solely seen in her assets or the high-quality education of her children. Her prowess was even recognised by NAFCOC. In 1973, she came second in the NAFCOC *"Businessman of the Year"* competition. The overall winner was Agrippa Mayaba, a wholesaler and bakery owner from Mt Frere in the Transkei.

22  Sapa report in Rand Daily Mail, "Trade Reflects Black Poverty", Thursday, November 25, 1971, p4
23  Author's interview with Luvuyo Peter Ntshona, June 14, 2023
24  Serache, N, Salesmen told: Be fair to Blacks, Rand Daily Mail, Tuesday, May 2, 1974, p19

Coming third was James Ngake, a supermarket owner in Welkom. Ntshona was somehow unimpressed with coming second. She believed the competition should have been grouped by business type, rather than being clustered by diverse sectors. She contended that she and other entrants were unfairly made to compete as retailers against a wholesaler and baker. The winner, Mayaba, employed 45 people in his bakery, which reportedly had a turnover of R150 000.

For the prize, he won a three-week educational trip to England. Ntshona also took a swipe at the national executive of NAFCOC, suggesting that they were biased towards business leaders in the homelands, as the Johannesburg branch was not in the good books of the NAFCOC leadership.[25]

*"I am not bitter because I have lost. I am only pointing out what I know goes on in our organisations,"* Ntshona would tell the *Rand Daily Mail.*

# How Ntshona's early life and the establishment of her business were shaped

Ntshona hailed from the Malunga lineage, *the Ndlovu's* of the Hlubi nation. She was born to a rather large family in Kimberley and pursued her studies in the Eastern Cape. After completing her studies at Lovedale Missionary Institute, she returned to Kimberley. As Luvuyo Ntshona recounted, she grew up as part of the emerging black middle class of the time. Her father, the tall and community-renowned Reuben Malunga, was a teacher and father of eight children. Ntshona was his second-eldest child.[26]

*" Reuben Malunga, **utat'omkhulu** (grandfather), was a teacher and had a prominent place in Kimberley society. I remember very well my childhood visits to his home at 399 Mzimba Street, Galeshewe . In her Kimberley days, nothing particularly stood out about my mother. Interestingly, my grandfather also ventured into business after he left teaching. He started a business in Kimberley, which still exists to this day and has been passed on to the younger generation. Perhaps this entrepreneurial spirit runs in our blood; we just did not realise it until much later," said Luvuyo.[27]*

25 Staff Reporter, Rand Daily Mail, "Row brews over business award", March 13, 1973, p22
26 Author's interview with Luvuyo Peter Ntshona, June 14, 2023
27 Ibid

The story goes that the then unmarried Constance "Connie" Malunga met Victor Scrape Ntshona – a stylish yet relatively short man – in Johannesburg. Connie was tall and quite attractive. Born in 1923, Scrape was two years senior to Constance.[28]

*"But my father was rather short. He was short in stature, but certainly not in confidence," narrated Luvuyo.[29]*

The Ntshonas, hailing from Mthatha, were well off and respected. Scrape's mother, Maria Ntshona (née Mxotwa), ran a boarding house on Madeira Street in Mthatha and was said to have been a very energetic woman.[30] The Ntshonas, of the Nkomoshe clan, originally came from Alice in Sheshegu. However, Scrape's father, John Wynne Ntshona, sought his fortune in Mthatha. Scrape attended the highly regarded missionary school, Healdtown, and then went on to finish his tertiary education at Fort Hare University.[31] At Fort Hare University, he completed a BSc degree.[32]

After his graduation, Scrape went to Cape Town, where he became involved in politics. He was part of the Unity Movement of South Africa, a Marxist-Leninist organisation. His political grounding, influenced by his stint at Fort Hare University, deepened in Cape Town. Subsequently, he moved to Johannesburg, where he taught at Fred Clarke, while Constance worked as a midwife at Jabavu Clinic in Soweto.[33]

Entrepreneurship didn't strike them instantly, recalled Luvuyo Ntshona. Upon settling in Johannesburg, they first sought a home, moving from White City to Dube; a new township at the time where owners could build their own houses. By 1956, they had established their residence at 1434 Pioneer Avenue in Dube Village.[34]

*"He had a young family to feed, and so the only way to begin to feed this young family was through entrepreneurship, if you will. Apart from that, he was beginning to become more active in Johannesburg, where he met the likes of Nelson [Mandela], [Robert] Resha," recalled Luvuyo, adding that his father was close to the then ANC President, Dr AB Xuma, and was best man at Mandela's wedding.[35]*

28  Ibid
29  Ibid
30  Author's interview with Dr Nokuzola Ntshona, June 14, 2023
31  Author's interview with Luvuyo Peter Ntshona, June 14, 2023
32  Rand Daily Mail, "Zola vows: I'll let no one down", Tuesday, August 10, 1971
33  Author's interview with Luvuyo Peter Ntshona, June 14, 2023
34  Ibid
35  Ibid

Scrape was fired from teaching in 1957 and was barred from teaching anywhere in the entire Republic. In the interim, between the end of his teaching career and 1959, the Ntshonas ventured into selling soft goods. By 1959, they had built the shop called People's Suppliers.[36]

*"We could not all live on the ideals of politics, nor could we subsist solely on my mother's meagre earnings as a midwife. So, they (my parents) built the shop in 1959. My mother left nursing and joined my father in this venture,"* Luvuyo explained.[37]

The *African Who's Who*, a biographical registry for notable figures in Transvaal, listed Victor Ntshona of Dube as a general dealer, operating from stands 307/08/09/10 in Zola.[38]

**Luvuyo recalled with pride:**

*" He built that store, a beautiful store in Zola, and named it People's Suppliers. We were very proud of that name because it reflected the values on both sides of our family – particularly my father's. It symbolised a commitment to serving and uplifting the community, a dedication to making lives better in places such as Zola."*[39]

However, Scrape's involvement in the business was short-lived. By 1963, the apartheid regime intensified its crackdown on progressive black individuals – many were incarcerated, others exiled, and political parties were banned. Scrape left, first finding refuge in Zambia before moving on to Nigeria.[40]

A passport application by Victor Ntshona reveals his intention to relocate to the Federation of Rhodesia for an indefinite period, to work at Anglo American Corporation in Lusaka.[41] However, the application was declined based on the *"Cabinet's decision not to allow qualified Bantu to leave the Republic".*[42]

The year 1963 also witnessed a significant crackdown on the ANC. The police raided the headquarters of uMkhonto we Sizwe, the military wing of the ANC. This led to the arrest of a number of ANC leaders, culminating in the infamous Rivonia Trial. Prominent ANC leaders, like Oliver Tambo and Joe Slovo, fled the country after avoiding arrest.[43]

36 Author's interview with Dr Nokuzola Ntshona, June 14, 2023
37 Author's interview with Luvuyo Peter Ntshona, June 14, 2023
38 Skota, M. The African Who's Who, An Illustrated Classified Register and National Biographical Dictionary of the Africans in the Transvaal, p335
39 Author's interview with Luvuyo Peter Ntshona, June 14, 2023
40 Ibid
41 National Archives of South Africa, BAO, Vol 3478, C100/6/736, The Secretary for the Bantu Administration and Development, Application for a Travel Document to Leave the Republic: Ntshona Victor Kunjulwe, 1963
42 National Archives of South Africa, BAO, Vol 3478, C100/6/736, Letter from Secretary for the Interior to The Secretary for Bantu Administration and Development, February 1, 1963
43 O'Malley Archive, https://omalley.nelsonmandela.org/index.php/site/q/03lv01538/04lv01539/05lv01551/06lv01555.htm

*"Immediately when that happened, my mother had to do something very quick. She had to stand up for her family, and that is when the entrepreneurial bug truly came to bear, because she now had to feed her two children. She took up the cudgels and took up the managerial position at People's Suppliers. My father only spent about four years in People's Suppliers and he was basically running the butchery more than anything. As I said things started getting hot at the turn of the [1960s]... That is when she became a true entrepreneur. She got to know people like Ephraim Tshabalala,"[44]* continued Luvuyo.

Ultimately, apartheid held her entrepreneurship spirit on its tracks. She ran the business until about 1978, almost 15 years after her husband, Scrape, had left for exile. Ntshona had endured difficult times, with her children and spouse out of the country.[45]

*"Apartheid was very gruelling on a singular woman; it was very gruelling. She had to find protection somehow. By 1977, having gone through the upheavals of '76, which were also gruelling, her store was not burnt, thank goodness. Many stores were burnt for no reason other than the fact that 'you are making more money than us'. That was the cruel paradox of apartheid; what it did to black businesspeople in the township,"* lamented Luvuyo.[46]

Luvuyo noted that apartheid was so bad for the black businessperson in the sense that many entrepreneurs were monitored by the security establishment. Their interactions and who they supported were constantly under scrutiny. At the same time, there were activists pressurising the black business community; questioning their profits, their lifestyles and choices, to send their children abroad.[47]

By 1977, Ntshona could not take it anymore. It was difficult for her, so she sold the business and moved to the US. Luvuyo believes her decision might have been influenced by the fact that her friends were also there. Luvuyo was also studying law in the US.[48]

[44] Author's interview with Luvuyo Peter Ntshona, June 14, 2023
[45] Ibid
[46] Ibid
[47] Ibid
[48] Ibid

The US was not completely foreign to Ntshona. In August 1974, she had visited the country and was presented with a golden plaque awarding her the freedom of the city for her activism and work as a woman in South Africa. The award had been given by the black District Mayor of Washington DC, Walter Washington. While there, Ntshona had addressed professional businesswomen in Philadelphia.[49]

When she moved to the US, Ntshona got an apartment in Washington DC. It had been hard dealing with apartheid spies watching her movements, on the one hand, and on the other, having to deal with the suspicion of her comrades, who could not understand her success, assuming it was because she was collaborating with the apartheid regime.[50] Her friend, John-Kane Berman, former chief executive of the South African Institute of Race Relations, wrote of how Constance Ntshona sheltered some of the students during the June 16, 1976 riots.[51]

Ntshona passed away in the US in 2006 and her friend and fellow businesswoman, Sally Motlana, spoke at the memorial service.[52]

# CONCLUSION

Constance Ntshona's legacy resonates far beyond the walls of her businesses; it stands out as an example of resilience during apartheid's darkest hours. Amidst racial biases and socio-economic roadblocks, she was not just a businesswoman; she was a trailblazer, challenging oppressive norms.

Her entrepreneurial acumen was matched only by her dedication to providing her children with unparalleled educational opportunities. Ntshona was more than a successful merchant; she was an advocate for equality, a voice against racial biases, and a testament to the indomitable spirit of women. Her legacy is a powerful reminder... even in history's oppressive chapters, sheer determination can craft tales of inspiration and enduring impact.

49  Rand Daily Mail, "Connie gets VIP Welcome in the USA", Tuesday, August 20, 1974, p26
50  Ibid
51  Kane-Berman, J, Business Day, "Constance Uncrushable: salute to a truly free spirit", p5
52  Ibid

# Sally Motlana

## The indomitable beacon of business and bravery

Sally Eva Motlana (née Maunye), also known simply as Mme Motlana, is counted as one of the formidable women in Soweto who ran a business amidst the oppressive and difficult backdrop of apartheid in the 1970s.

Mme Motlana began her foray into business in the early 1960s. In October 1962, there was an advert announcing that one Lazarus Nxumalo, who ran Cross Roads Restaurant and Butchery located at stand 1330/1, Mofolo Central, Soweto, was selling his business. On October 24, 1962, Mme Motlana took over the business, operating it from the same address *"for her own account and benefit"*.[1]

As far back as 1972, the press recognised Mme Motlana as a *"prominent Soweto businesswoman"*.[2] She also ran a shop called Sizwe Store in Mofolo Central, which she continued to manage well into the new millennium.[3]

There is another facet to the story – that Sizwe Store was opened with the assistance of Mme Motlana's husband, the famous Dr Ntatho Harrison Motlana. Being a medical doctor-turned-political activist, he frequently endured harassment and arrests by agents of the apartheid regime due to his political activities. So, he thought it prudent to establish the store, so that his family did not struggle during periods of his incarceration. The management of the business then fell on Mme Motlana.[4]

1   Rand Daily Mail, "Notice of Alienation of Business", Tuesday October 23, 1962, p14
2   Staff Reporter, Rand Daily Mail, "Church leader is in hospital", Tuesday January 18, 1972, p5
3   Xaba, P, Sowetan, "Viva Women of Africa Viva", December 12, 2002, p22
4   Sowetan, "Dr Motlana will Phola in Johannesburg", August 25, 2004, p28

While acknowledging her husband's involvement, Mme Motlana underscored the point that she was in charge and emphasised her leadership role in the business. In a call for women to be given more opportunities in business, Mme Motlana was once quoted in the *Rand Daily Mail* as saying:

*"Businesses would be run more efficiently and in better spirit, if women conducted the sales. We have proved it to our husbands who have left us to run the shops."*[5]

Born from humble beginnings and difficult circumstances, Sally Motlana was a self-made businesswoman. She was born in Moremela, near Pilgrim's Rest in present-day Mpumalanga Province. Due to inadequate record-keeping at the time of her birth, she is said to have given herself the date of birth of April 9, 1927.[6] This date was later celebrated as her official birthday.[7]

It is believed that Mme Motlana was only a baby when she travelled from her birthplace to Johannesburg, carried on her mother's back. In Johannesburg, the family settled in Sophiatown, where Mme Motlana attended school at St Cyprian's Anglican Church in Sophiatown; Western Native High School (later known as Madibane High School). She then attended the Diocesan (Teacher) Training College in Pietersburg (now Polokwane). While teaching, she completed her matric through Lyceum College in 1949, and thereafter graduated with a BA degree from the University of Fort Hare in 1952.

It was during her time at Fort Hare that she joined the ANC Youth League (ANCYL), and was later elected secretary of the ANCYL Fort Hare branch. This period also marked her acquaintance with Dr Nthato Motlana, leading to a marriage, which blessed them with a daughter and three sons. Because of the introduction of the flawed Bantu education system, she decided to quit her teaching career.[8]

5    Staff Reporter, Rand Daily Mail, "Women want responsibility", Saturday, September 24, 1966, p3
6    Beltramo, C. The Star, "The bitterness I feel- by Sally Motlana", March 24, 1981
7    Funeral Service of the struggle stalwart and anti-apartheid activist Sally Motlana,
     https://www.youtube.com/watch?v=-Ogiz4AwCHI.w
8    Xaba, P, Sowetan, "Viva Women of Africa Viva", December 12, 2002, p22

Mme Motlana was active in the community, and it was not uncommon to see her alongside esteemed business leaders, like Sam Motsuenyane, at National African Chamber of Commerce (NAFCOC) conference halls.[9]

However, her journey was not without challenges. Her business operations were often disrupted by the apartheid security agents, who conducted raids targeting political activism. This highlighted the notion that the resistance against apartheid itself posed a significant barrier to black economic advancement.

During the tumultuous Soweto riots of June 16, 1976, her shop became a hiding place for several youths. She would tell her biographer, Mukoni Ratshitanga, of a harrowing incident when armed police pursued students into her shop. When the police tried to enter the store to apprehend the youngsters, it was Mme Motlana who determinedly stood her ground, refusing them entry.[10]

9    Tshabalala, R. Rand Daily Mail Extra, "Sally Motlana with Prof Henry Joannies of Paris, Betty Hirzel, Chairman of the South African Consumer Union", Monday March 19, 1984
10   Ratshitanga, M, "Don't Polish my Chains- farewell to Sally Motlana", https://www.timeslive.co.za/sunday-times-daily/opinion-and-analysis/2023-06-29-mukoni-ratshitanga-dont-polish-my-chains-farewell-to-sally-motlana/

In 1976, both Mme Motlana, who also held the position of vice-president of the South African Council of Churches, and her husband, Dr Ntatho Motlana, were arrested under the Internal Security Act, leading to a five-month detention. Then in February 1977, Mme Motlana found herself in custody once again, this time under the Terrorism Act.[11] In 1978, Mme Motlana faced yet another arrest, resulting in nearly two months of detention. This left her children to oversee and manage the shop in her absence.[12]

In the 1970s, Mme Motlana was a dynamic force and held the esteemed position of national president of the Black Housewives' League for 20 years. Her dedication and leadership eventually earned her the title of honorary president of the organisation. It was under her leadership

that Black Housewives' League was involved in significant projects, such as building a six-classroom primary school in Polokwane.

The organisation also secured land to grow vegetables. Other vegetable projects were also established in areas outside Polokwane, such as Lebowakgomo, Bushbuckridge and Kiblaren. The Black Housewives' League also built a crèche in 1989, with more to follow.[13]

By the 1980s, Mme Sally Motlana was already a voice of advocacy and change. As a leader of the Black Housewives' League, she spoke out against the authorities' unjust treatment of black pensioners, who often had to stand in long queues in harsh weather conditions to receive their pensions.

She staunchly believed that black pensioners should also enjoy the same convenience of collecting their pensions at the Post Office, which their white, coloured and Indian counterparts enjoyed.[14]

With the dawn of democracy in South Africa, Mme Motlana's business prospects expanded. In 1997, she was appointed as a non-executive director of JSE-listed sawmilling company Yorkcor.[15] In its report to shareholders in 2006, Yorkcor expressed profound gratitude to Mme Motlana, lauding her for her invaluable "insights and guidance" to the company. She sat on Yorkcor's Remuneration Board Committee.[16]

Sadly, Mme Motlana passed away on Saturday, June 24, 2023, at the venerable age of 96.[17]

[11] Staff Reporter, Rand Daily Mail, "Church leader held under Terror Act", Wednesday February 23, 1977, p3
[12] Sisulu, Z, Rand Daily Mail, "Sally released from Solitary", Wednesday December 20, 1978
[13] Profile of Sally Motlana, The Order of the Baobab in Silver, https://www.thepresidency.gov.za/national-orders/recipient/sally-motlana-1927
[14] Rand Daily Mail, "The aged defy the elements in a long vigil to collect their R66 pensions", March 13, 1961, p3
[15] Yorkcor Annual Report 2005, p21
[16] Yorkcor Annual Report 2006, p11-14
[17] President mourns passing of veteran activist Mam Sally Motlana, June 25, 2023, https://www.thepresidency.gov.za/press-statements/president-mourns-passing-veteran-activist-mam-sally-motlana

# CONCLUSION

Throughout her life, Mme Motlana stood as a beacon of resilience, leadership, and unwavering commitment to justice and community upliftment. From her influential role in the Black Housewives' League to her advocacy for the rights of black pensioners, her endeavours consistently aimed to elevate the status of those marginalised under apartheid.

As an entrepreneur, she faced adversity head-on, skillfully navigating the complexities of both business and activism during South Africa's tumultuous era. In her later years, her business acumen was recognised and sought-after in the mainstream economy, illustrating the depth of her impact across various sectors. Mme Motlana's life story is not just a testament to her personal strength, but also a reflection of the indomitable spirit of countless women who fought against the odds in a deeply divided nation.

# Epainette Mbeki

Getty Images: Epainette Mbeki, Rhodes University's graduation ceremony on April 13, 2012

## A legacy of resilience, community service and empowerment

Epainette Mbeki, better known as *"MaMbeki"*, was notably the only businessperson with the title *"Mrs"* registered as a delegate at the inaugural National African Chamber of Commerce (NAFCOC) conference in April 1964. In the minutes and list of 66 registered delegates noted to have been present at the NAFCOC conference in April 1964, MaMbeki's name was recorded as the 34th delegate on the register. She was one of four people from the Transkei at a meeting largely dominated by businessmen from the Transvaal.[1]

*At the time of the 1964 conference, MaMbeki ran a shop in the rural area of Mbewuleni in Dutywa, in the Transkei. The business had been started in the 1940s and MaMbeki had been left with the responsibility of control as her husband, Govan "Oom Gov" Mbeki, criss-crossed the country engaged in political work. And when he was at home, Oom Gov was in the study writing. MaMbeki had to operate the shop and raise her children Linda, Thabo, Moeletsi and Jama.[2]*

1 Kondlo, K. (2014). A Legacy of Perseverance, NAFCOC: 50 Years of Leadership in Business, p14
2 Gevisser, M. (2022). Thabo Mbeki: The Dream Deferred, Updated International Edition, p34

Oom Gov's journalism work did not generate much income for the Mbeki household, which had to be enhanced through merchant activities such as livestock. MaMbeki was baking scones and cakes for a coffee shop and when Oom Gov left the editorial team of Inkundla, the family relied on the shop.[3]

The business grew and even sold over-the-counter medicine like painkillers, cough mixture, castor oil and teething powders. For a general dealer's licence, the Mbekis paid £3 and £2 to sell patent medicine. The business grew to sell blankets, bags of maize, and agricultural equipment. The shop operated a postal service where letters were read and written for members of the community.[4]

*According to Colin Bundy, the idea of starting the business had been ignited by Oom Gov's "political enthusiasm" and an interest in cooperatives. He was influenced by his academic pursuits while studying for his Bachelor of Commerce degree and had also read Father Bernard Huss's work on cooperative self-help. So, a cooperative store was started.[5]*

Oom Gov had also been involved in the Cooperative Credit Societies in the Transkei led by the venerable Charles Kwelemthini (CK) Sakwe. At a meeting attended by Oom Gov in Engcobo on February 24, 1940, alongside RS Zwakala and Chief Poswa, a financial report

was delivered. It advised that the assets of the society were close to £2000, and a good deal of the amount had been advanced to members in loans and there was £126-8-5 left in actual cash.[6] It is not clear if the credit society had also loaned cash to the Mbekis to start the business.

Gevisser wrote that with money lent by comrades, Oom Gov supervised the construction of a large five-roomed house in Mbewuleni, which included a shop at the back. The home had a garden where corn, cabbages, and tomatoes were planted. A prickly pear border was created by MaMbeki to discourage stray cattle and goats from infiltrating the garden.[7]

*The cooperative aspect of the store dwindled as other partners dropped out, leaving the business under the control of the Mbekis.[8]*

Initially, the Mbekis had wanted to start the business in a higher traffic area occupied by African Christians, but some white shop owners objected, complaining that this would be in violation of a rule prohibiting the opening of a business within five miles of a white-owned business. So, the Mbekis had to set up their shop on the traditional side of the amaqaba (red ochred), who were not the strongest believers in Christianity.[9]

The strategic location of white-owned trading sites in African Christian communities was underscored by the activist Phyllis Ntantala, who grew up in Dutywa. She highlighted that

3   Mbeki, G. (1991). Learning from Robben Island: The Prison Writings of Govan Mbeki, Introduction by Colin Bundy, pxiv
4   Gevisser, M. (2022). Thabo Mbeki. The Dream Deferred, Updated International Edition, p34
5   Mbeki, G. (1991). Learning from Robben Island, The Prison Writings of Govan Mbeki, Introduction by Colin Bundy, pxv
6   The Territorial Magazine, The Annual Report, Co-operative Credit Societies, March 1940, p2
7   Gevisser, M. (2022). Thabo Mbeki, The Dream Deferred, Updated International Edition, p34
8   Mbeki, G. (1991). Learning from Robben Island: The Prison Writings of Govan Mbeki, Introduction by Colin Bundy, pxiv
9   Gevisser, M. (2022). Thabo Mbeki The Dream Deferred, Updated International Edition, p32

white traders had come to the Transkei "hot on the heels of the missionaries, to provide all the new needs that missionaries demanded and to satisfy the new tastes that had been introduced".[10] Ntantala would write that for Africans to be accepted as Christians, they had to wear European clothing, which they could only get from the traders, and included food items such as tea, coffee, sugar, flour, as well as objects such as pots, ploughs and dishes that the Western and non-Western educated populations fell for.[11]

When the business was started, the Mbekis had moved to the Transkei after teaching in Natal. A 2012 citation for the conferment of an honorary Doctorate in Law, indicated that MaMbeki, born in 1916, had studied at Mariazell in Matatiele, then Lovedale College in Alice and Adams College in Amanzimtoti, and graduated as a schoolteacher. In the late 1930s, she took up a teaching post in Durban at Taylor Street Secondary School, and there she met fellow teacher and future husband, Oom Gov. In Durban, MaMbeki started getting involved in community work and activism, which she continued for over seven decades. Professor Paul Maylam wrote that it was in the Transkei that MaMbeki made her mark after moving back there, to Mbewuleni, after their marriage in 1940.[12]

*The marriage records of Govan and Epainette Mbeki show that the couple got married on January 8, 1940, in Mt Fletcher, Cape Province. Oom Gov was 29 years old and MaMbeki was 23.[13]*

It was during a marriage season of high-flyers that even caught the attention of *The Territorial Magazine* of January 1940. Among the list of couples that were publicised for getting married during the holidays of December 1939 to January 1940 were Archibald Campbell Jordan, an academic (a Bachelor of Arts graduate) from Tsolo, and Phyllis Ntantala from Dutywa; Govan Mbeki (a Bachelor of Arts graduate from Ngqamakwe) and Epainette Mbeki from Mt Fletcher; Harvey Ntloko Yako (a Bachelor of Arts graduate from Mqanduli) and Beatrice Tyamzashe from Kimberley.[14]

It was not smooth sailing for MaMbeki as her journey as a trader was fraught with challenges. In 1954, a tornado tore apart the roof of the shop, destroying the inventory. The natural disaster happened a day after MaMbeki had returned from Dutywa with remittances from migrant labourers to their families. These were also destroyed, leaving the Mbekis indebted to customers. In 1955, a fire further damaged the shop. The Mbekis had no insurance. One of the challenges faced by the Mbekis was supply chain constraints. Oom Gov had lost income after falling out with his political comrades and resigning from the Bhunga council. An attempt to expand the business by opening a store in a neighbouring village and a tearoom in Dutywa also failed.[15]

In addition, apartheid had brought unhappiness and disintegration to the Mbeki family. Oom Gov was away from home, involved in national political campaigns, and was arrested and sentenced to life imprisonment at the Rivonia Trial in 1964. MaMbeki's three sons were in exile, and

10   Ntantala, P. (1993). A Life's Mosaic: The Autobiography of Phyllis Ntantala, p4
11   Ibid
12   Maylam, P., Citation for Epainette Mbeki, Honorary graduand, Rhodes University, April 13, 2012. See also https://www.thepresidency.gov.za/epaulette-mbeki-1916
13   "South Africa, Civil Marriage Records, 1840-1973", FamilySearch (https://www.familysearch.org/ark:/61903/1:1:6ZHB-DLXK : Fri Oct 20 09:01:12 UTC 2023), Entry for Govan Archibald Mbeki and Epainette Moerane, 8 Jan 1940
14   The Territorial Magazine, Abatshatileyo, January 1940
15   Gevisser, M, Thabo Mbeki The Dream Deferred, Updated International Edition, p41

she faced numerous police raids on her home, even during the middle of the night with the security people seizing her notes, family pictures, and what was left of the disintegrated family. She soldiered on and even paid Oom Gov's study fees.[16]

In his Presidential Address on May 20, 1967, Zwelinjani Conco, the second president of NAFCOC, a garage proprietor and store owner in Natal, noted that circumstances beyond the control of business leaders in the Transkei had forced them to identify with political parties, and this affected the progress of the chamber in that homeland. Conco stated that as a result, NAFCOC's national committee had to tread cautiously in the Transkei.[17]

*In 1974, MaMbeki moved out of Mbewuleni to Ngcingwane, in Dutywa, a village closer to town. There, she set up shop again and engaged in community activities. She grew and sold vegetables, and in 1982 was secretary and treasurer of the Dutywa agricultural show. She helped the community to get a site for a school.[18]*

After 1994, as a businesswoman and the mother of South Africa's then Deputy President (Thabo Mbeki), MaMbeki was not immune to societal ills. In 1997, gun-wielding criminals robbed her of money at the shop in Ngcingwane.[19] The episode was followed by reports that MaMbeki was closing the doors of her "Goodwill" store, due to the crime incident.[20]

*However, in 1999, when Thabo Mbeki ascended to become President of South Africa, media outlets described MaMbeki, then 83 years old, as an operator of a shop.[21]*

In 2006 President Mbeki awarded MaMbeki, the Order of the Baobab in gold, for her contribution to the economic upliftment of underprivileged communities in the Eastern Cape and the fight against apartheid. She was praised for organising the women of her village into a craft and beadwork cooperative called Khanyisa.[22]

## MaMbeki passed away in 2014 at the age of 98.[23]

16  Gevisser, M, Thabo Mbeki The Dream Deferred, Updated International Edition. p41
17  Maylam, P, Citation for Epainette Mbeki, Honorary graduand, Rhodes University, April 13, 2012[17] Presidential Address Delivered by the President Mr S.Z Conco, At the Third Annual Conference of the National African Chamber of Commerce, Held at Cape Town, May 20, 1967
18  Maylam, P, Citation for Epainette Mbeki, Honorary graduand, Rhodes University, April 13, 2012
19  South African Press Association (SAPA) cited in The Star, Mbeki's mother robbed at her shop, November 18, 1997, p1
20  Macgregor, D, Thabo Mbeki's mother shuts up shop after armed robbery, Saturday Argus, November 23, 1997, p3
21  SAPA cited in The Star, Mother readying for inauguration, June 7, 1999, p7
22  Order of the Baobab in gold, https://www.thepresidency.gov.za/epaulette-mbeki-1916
23  South African Broadcasting Corporation, Funeral Service of Epainette Mbeki, https://www.youtube.com/watch?v=ASLYpMEBeYE

# WOMEN THRIVING
## IN BUSINESS AGAINST ALL ODDS

Despite the constraints imposed on black traders, black businesswomen arguably faced even greater structural barriers inhibiting their entrepreneurial potential. Yet, these challenges did not deter them from working hard and fighting to occupy male-dominated spaces.

In the late 1960s, Lettie Mabasa of Mamelodi nearly lost her dairy business following her husband's death. Officials from the Pretoria Non-European Affairs Department threatened to revoke the business's trading licence. The patriarchy was so opposed to Mrs Mabasa's business interests that when she tried to appeal to the Bantu Affairs Commissioner, she was told that her business could only continue if her son was 18 or older. Her son was still a minor at the time. This stipulation had significant implications for many family businesses without a male heir above 18 years.

Nevertheless, Mrs Mabasa did not quit. Her tenacity forced the Mamelodi Advisory Board to approach the Bantu Commissioner on her behalf.[1]

Two months after this intervention, the authorities allowed Mrs Mabasa to continue with the business, even though her son had not reached the age of 18. However, this was after the legality of her marriage was questioned due to the absence of documentary evidence confirming its legitimacy.[2]

The discriminatory regulations against women were not limited to Mamelodi. In 1971, when Soweto businesswoman, Constance Ntshona, campaigned to be in the Urban Bantu Council in Soweto, she vowed to fight against regulations denying women, especially widows, the right to register as tenants of houses in Soweto.[3]

[1] Staff Reporter, Rand Daily Mail, "Board May Help Widow", Thursday, March 6, 1969, p5
[2] Staff Reporter, Rand Daily Mail, "Widow Can Carry on Business", Thursday, June 5, 1969, p5
[3] Staff Reporter, Rand Daily Mail, "Women's Lib at polls", Friday, September 3, 1971, p5

Another prevailing stereotype and struggle that black businesswomen faced at the time was that they were always perceived as proxies of their husbands. Challenging this narrative, Dorothy Tsolo, a 32-year-old mother of two who ran a general dealer in Rockville, Soweto, quipped in 1979:

*"I'm on my own. I run the business while my husband works as a clerk in the city."* [4]

Dinah Meleke, another businesswoman from Diepkloof, Soweto, echoed similar sentiments. She pointed out that she managed the purchases for the shop she co-ran with her husband. [5]

*"You must be able to do things on your own – take over and keep things running smoothly if your husband is not there,"* Meleke, a mother of three, would insist.

Before becoming a businesswoman, Tsolo initially worked as a receptionist, and later as a switchboard operator. She then opened a modest shop in Dobsonville in 1976. After almost two years, she grew the business into a comprehensive general dealership in Rockville, Soweto, selling groceries, toiletries, stationery and hardware. [6]

To improve their acumen in business, both Tsolo and Meleke prioritised continual learning. In 1979, they attended a five-day business programme, aimed at improving their retail business experience. This course, run by the Centre for Developing Business in Soweto, was sponsored by the Coca-Cola Company. One of the primary objectives of the programme was to educate shop owners on better retail planning and effective cashflow management. [7]

Balancing her roles as a mother and businesswoman, Tsolo was unapologetic and publicly outspoken about the importance of men doing unpaid care work. Running the General Dealer necessitated her to start the day early, often leaving home by 6:00am. [8]

4    Stevens, S, Rand Daily Mail, "Making plans for the future", October 5, 1979, p9
5    Stevens, S, Rand Daily Mail, "Making plans for the future", October 5, 1979, p9
6    Stevens, S, Rand Daily Mail, "Making plans for the future", October 5, 1979, p9
7    Stevens, S, Rand Daily Mail, "Making plans for the future", October 5, 1979, p9
8    Rand Daily Mail, January 24, 1980, p5

*"Some husbands think that when they come home, they have to sit down and let the wife do everything. But I can't keep up to date with the housekeeping on my own. We must help each other as partners. My husband and I work hand-in-hand. If he gets home before me, he does the cooking. He used to help bath and dress the children when they were smaller,"* elaborated Tsolo.

*"During the school terms, my husband gives our daughter breakfast, sees that she's washed and dressed properly and drops her at school. If a wife stays at home, it's not necessary for the man to help so much. But if you both work, you have to help each other."* [9]

The efforts made by businesswomen such as Tsolo, Meleke, Constance Ntshona, Epainette Mbeki, Sally Motlana, Catherine Gadi and countless others, illustrate the capability of women to run businesses in the absence of male counterparts. These examples offer merely a glimpse of what women can achieve in commerce, given the right conditions.

[9]   Rand Daily Mail, January 24, 1980. p5

# Leso

A JOURNEY FROM EDUCATOR TO ENTREPRENEUR

"

# SJJ
# lang

A founding director of African Bank, Lesolang was Treasurer of NAFCOC, the organisation that collected money to start African Bank.[1] As Treasurer he would often struggle with people who made deposits without disclosing their names and addresses. This made Lesolang's life quite difficult, as it became almost impossible to acknowledge some of the depositors.[2]

Solomon Joel Jack (SJJ) Lesolang, a pioneer and influential figure in both the education and business sectors of South Africa, was born on October 2, 1906, in Sambokstad, Pretoria.[3]

His educational journey, which began at St Cyprian's School, was supplemented by a correspondence course that furnished him with both junior and senior certificates. After training as an educator at the Diocesan Training College, Pietersburg, Lesolang embarked on a teaching career in 1928 until 1945. He would later transition from education to business in a remarkable way, culminating in his ascension to the role of Treasurer of the National Federated Chamber of Commerce (NAFCOC). His efforts were recognised with an honorary life membership of the chamber, marking his valuable contribution to the organisation.[4]

1   UNISA Archives, ACC290, Who is the Treasurer, Report by PG Gumede, Vice President Nafcoc, June 17, 1974, p3.
2   UNISA Archives, ACC290, NAFCOC Minutes of the Ninth Annual Conference Held at Mafeking, May17-20, 1973, p5
3   UNISA Archives, ACC290, Who is the Treasurer, Report by PG Gumede, Vice President Nafcoc, June 17, 1974, p3.
4   UNISA Archives, ACC290, Who is the Treasurer, Report by PG Gumede, Vice President Nafcoc, June 17, 1974, p3.

A socially conscious leader, Lesolang dedicated significant time in the early years of his career to the welfare of his fellow educators. He served as Vice President of the Transvaal African Teacher's Association (TATA) from 1938 to 1942 and ascended to its presidency in 1942 until 1945.[5] During this period, he taught at Geduld School on the Reef in Johannesburg, where he also held the position of head teacher.[6]

During his time in TATA leadership, Lesolang developed and maintained a close relationship with the highly esteemed African National Congress President-General, Dr Alfred Bitini (AB) Xuma. Together, they would often engage on matters affecting the educational welfare of Africans and the compensation of teachers.[7] Due to his dedication towards education, Lesolang was appointed as a member of a deputation composed of notable figures such as ZK Matthews, Professor DDT Jabavu, AC Jordan, RH Godlo and JD Rheinallt Jones. The deputation was tasked with engaging government on matters related to Native education.[8]

At its July 1945 conference held at Emmarentia in Johannesburg, TATA appointed Lesolang as a full-time secretary of the organisation with a fixed salary. During this period, TATA leased an office at the Progress Building in Johannesburg (156 Commissioner Street), and a clerk was employed to assist him. By 1946, however, the cost of maintaining this arrangement led to the termination of his full-time role.[9]

Wits Historical Papers Research Archive: SJJ Lesolang

Wits Historical Papers Research Archive, AD2523, South African Institute of Race Relations, Collections of Publications, TATA 60th Anniversary, May 1966, p12-13
Wits Historical Papers Research Archive, AD1715, South African Institute of Race Relations, Diocese of Johannesburg, Anglican Primary Schools, Witwatersrand Area, 1938 Review,
Wits Historical Papers Research Archive, ABX4204309, Letter from AB Xuma to SJJ Lesolang, March 9, 1942
Wits Historical Papers Research Archive, ABX430708, Native Education, July 29, 1943, p4
Wits Historical Papers Research Archive, AD2523, South African Institute of Race Relations, Collections of Publications, TATA 60th Anniversary, May 1966, p12-13

Beyond his contributions to education, Lesolang was a respected leader and resident of Soweto. He soon gained the recognition as one of Johannesburg's most progressive Africans. He was a founding member of the National Chamber of Commerce (NACOC), previously known as African Chamber of Commerce, which later evolved into NAFCOC.[10]

Armed with a diploma in Commerce from Cape Town Commercial College, when Lesolang left teaching, he became a director in his family's business, Rantol (Pty) Ltd, which had been established in the early 1940s. The birth of Rantol (Pty) Ltd marked the inception of a series of enterprises, including Itekeng Syndicate (Pty) Ltd in 1952, Rantol Motors (Pty) Ltd in 1959, Tlhaseng Enterprises Ltd, Moutse Enterprises (Pty) Ltd, Lesolang Coal Agency (Pty) Ltd, and Ga-Rankuwa Wood and Coal Distributors.[11]

With its headquarters in Orlando, Soweto, Itekeng Syndicate (Pty) Ltd was a coal and wood distribution company founded in 1952. Embracing the motto *"Prompt execution of Order"*, Itekeng Syndicate acted as an intermediary, supplying coal to the townships and retailers from the Orlando and Nancefield stations. The coal was sourced from places such as Witbank.[12] As townships did not have electricity, Itekeng was filling a gap in the market, providing the energy resource used for cooking and heating, and other purposes.[13]

In a 1955 interview with *Bantu World* newspaper, Lesolang explained that Itekeng sold to retailers who in turn vended from house to house. By 1955, Itekeng had eight coal sites and supplied 4 500 tons of coal to African communities annually. However, the company faced challenges. There were reports of complaints that while Europeans had no difficulty in selling their coal, the African coal merchants faced restrictions as they had to apply for permits and find suitable coal sites. These were restrictions that European coal dealers did not encounter.[14]

Doing business was never easy; the Lesolang family faced challenges with their Rantol Bus Service. Named after Lesolang's brother, George Rantol Lesolang, the service operated routes from Orlando West II and Elizabethville, largely the area between Meadowlands and Orlando Station in Soweto.[15] On March 1, 1955, however, the Local Road Transportation Board rejected an application by Rantol Bus Service to operate its existing route. Instead, a motor carrier certificate was granted to the Public Utility Transport Corporation (PUTCO). In response, the Rantol company engaged Mandela & Tambo Attorneys to contest the decision. The case was subsequently assigned to Oliver Tambo.[16]

[10] Wits Historical Papers Research Archive, A1618, TD Mweli Skota Papers, African Yearly Register, African Who's Who
[11] UNISA Archives, ACC290, Who Is the Treasurer, Report by PG Gumede, Vice President Nafcoc, June 17, 1974, p3
[12] Wits Historical Papers Research Archive, A1132-Cl3 Patrick Robert Brian Lewis Papers, Mohloding Vol 2, 1968
[13] Wits Historical Papers Research Archive, Bantu World, Townships must get coal, October 16, 1954, p3
[14] Wits Historical Papers Research Archive, Bantu World, December 24, 1955, p1
[15] See My Heritage, https://www.myheritage.com/names/george_lesolang
[16] National Archives of South Africa VER, DAI8/5/1502, Appeal Mandela and Tambo (Rantol Bus Service) Against the Decision of Local Road Transportation Board Johannesburg, 1955, p5–6

In the appeal, Tambo noted that Rantol Bus Service was only informed of the application's rejection through a letter dated March 14, 1955, yet the company did not receive this notice until March 16, 1955. He further argued that the carrier certificate awarded to PUTCO was identical to the one previously used by the Rantol Bus Service, save for a negligible difference in distance between Elizabethville and Meadowlands, which suggested the preferential treatment that white-owned operators were given over their black counterparts.

Tambo would aver that there had been no indication that Rantol was providing an unsatisfactory service. He argued that the Local Road Transportation Board should have been promoting passenger carrier services owned by black people in the Orlando area. Tambo further suggested that the denial of Rantol's application reflected a policy intended to undermine the company and cause financial harm. Despite their fervent arguments, Mandela and Tambo were unable to make significant progress and eventually withdrew the appeal.[17] As a result, the Lesolangs decided to exit the passenger transport industry and reportedly sold their business to PUTCO.[18]

The Rantol incident was not the first incident where PUTCO had been accused of receiving preferential treatment at the expense of a black bus operator. Established in 1945 by Jack Bird Barregar, following bus-boycotts in Johannesburg, PUTCO enjoyed government subsidies.[19]

This was perceived as a distinct advantage to PUTCO over black-owned bus operators, who did not receive such support.

During the 1950s, Lesolang also experienced a personal challenge, namely the split from his wife Sophia. He called on Mandela & Tambo Attorneys to handle the matter.[20]

As a leading figure in a group that wanted to oust Paul Ramotsoane Mosaka, the then African Chamber of Commerce President, Lesolang was also served with a £111 bill in 1956 for leading the costly litigation, at the Supreme Court in the Witwatersrand. In a letter dated March 5, 1958, the Acting Deputy Sheriff of Johannesburg would later report that Lesolang had made a full settlement to Mosaka's attorneys.[21] It is not clear if Lesolang bore the cost alone, as he had consorted with other businessmen in attempts to remove Mosaka.

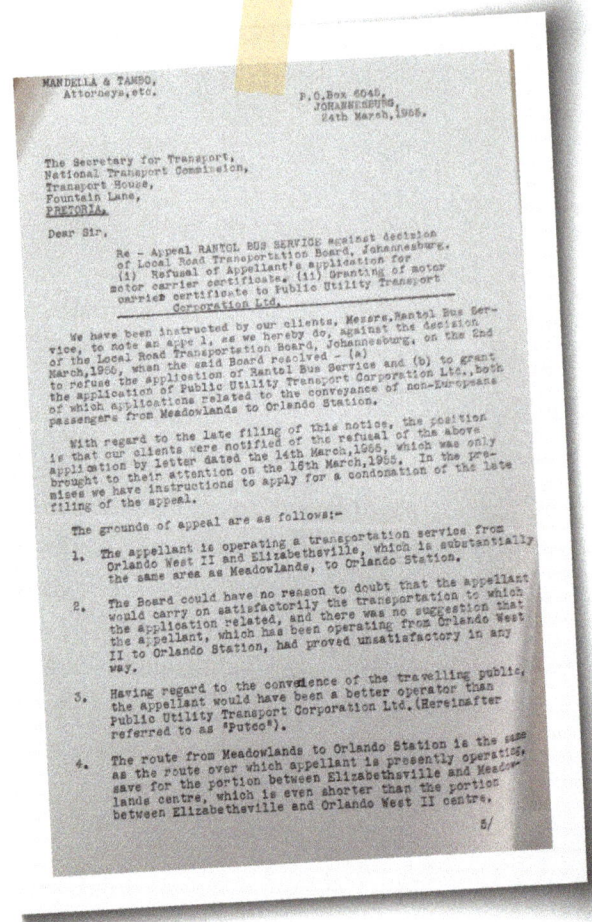

National Archives of South Africa: VER, DA18/5/1502

[17] National Archives of South Africa VER DA18/5/1502, Appeal Mandela and Tambo (Rantol Bus Service) Against the Decision of Local Road Transportation Board Johannesburg, 1955, p5-6
[18] Mojapelo, JS, He forged an empire on the lessons of protest, Rand Daily Mail, February 5, 1981, p11
[19] Stadler, A, 1987, The Political Economy of Modern South Africa, p126
[20] National Archives of South Africa, SEJ 373/56, Divorce, Solomon Joel Jack Lesolang versus Sophia Lydin Lesolang
[21] National Archives of South Africa, WLD 985/1956, Opposed Application, Solomon Joel Jack Lesolang versus Paul Ramotsoane Mosaka, 1956

Papers filed in 1956 showed that Lesolang, then described as a shopkeeper in Orlando West, had lodged an application together with Walter Stanford Pela, a shopkeeper in Orlando West; Stephen Mncube, a shopkeeper in Dube village; Ben Jacob Mabuza, Alexander Bootie Mathobela; Ephraim Robert Tshabalala, a shopkeeper in Mofolo; White Dirapelo Mpolokeng from the Abyssinian Supply Store; Petrus Kasas (PK) Seabela and Peter Motemekoane Lengene.

All nine applicants were executive committee members of the African Chamber of Commerce (ACOC), and had filed a case against their president, Mosaka, a shopkeeper and operator of Goodwill Burial Society. Pela, who was ACOC secretary at the time, had been suspended by Mosaka for allegedly neglecting his duties, displaying insubordination, and spreading mischievous propaganda. However, Mosaka's executive sided with Pela and retaliated against what they deemed a unilateral decision. Mosaka was accused of overstepping his powers on a matter that required the collective action of the executive. Furthermore, Mosaka was accused of causing ACOC to receive less money from donors due to alleged interference.[22] Though the matter was brought before the Supreme Court, there was a sentiment that it could have been settled through discussion at an ACOC meeting.

Mandela & Tambo Attorneys instructed Advocate Jack Unterhalter to conduct a meeting to resolve the dispute between the ACOC executive committee and its president outside the court process.

However, that meeting descended into chaos due to disagreement about credentials and eligibility of who could attend. There was also a walk-out by the members of the executive opposing Mosaka.[23] Justice Kuper of the Supreme Court opined that bringing such a dispute to court was wasteful, given that it could have been resolved by the members of ACOC themselves.[24]

Despite the numerous challenges he faced in the courts and in his business ventures during the 1950s, Lesolang would ultimately rise to prominence as a respected business leader in apartheid-era South Africa.

Reflecting on Lesolang's entrepreneurial journey, the veteran business reporter JS [John] Mojapelo of the *Rand Daily Mail* recalled that Lesolang's family had started selling coal in Orlando 1945 with limited capital and business experience. Despite running at a loss in their first year, they did not give up. As their business interests grew, they acquired a trading licence in the Free State, ventured into bus services, established a cargo transport business, opened general dealer shops, garages, a butchery and coal businesses. It was after the battles with PUTCO in the 1950s that the Lesolang family started the cargo transport business in 1959. They delivered ash and cement during the housing construction peak in Soweto. However, when their contract unexpectedly ended two years later, the Rantol business was stranded with eleven costly trucks and outstanding bills.

22 Ibid
23 Ibid
24 Ibid

The increasingly difficult trading conditions in black urban areas, due to government laws, prompted the Lesolang family to move back to Ga-Rankuwa in the homeland of Bophuthatswana in 1962. Throughout the 1960s, Lesolang became a prominent voice advocating for traders' rights through NAFCOC. He entered politics in Bophuthatswana as a rival to Lucas Mangope, but retired in 1977. Lesolang's business ventures flourished and by the 1970s, he had grown his enterprise to sell brand-new cars through a franchise.[25]

In 1980, he won the NAFCOC Businessman of the Year award in recognition of running a business with an annual turnover of over R500 000.[26] This accolade afforded him the opportunity to undertake a business experience trip to the US, where he visited black-controlled businesses, banks, and financial institutions. While in the US, he also sought insights on how to raise funds for NAFCOC's ambitious retail project, the Black Chain.[27]

Lesolang served as chairman of Black Chain, a NAFCOC initiative aimed at entering the retail commercial property and mega supermarket market in a significant way. The project included doctor's rooms, speciality shops and cash-and-carry warehouses. Capital for its construction was raised through issuing shares to black individuals and securing funding from financial institutions.[28]

Lesolang retired from business in 1987. He passed away at the age of 88 in 1995 and was survived by his wife, Rosa, and children.[29]

# HIS STORY SERVES AS AN ENDURING BEACON OF INSPIRATION FOR ASPIRING ENTREPRENEURS AND LEADERS

25 Mojapelo, JS. 'He forged an empire on the lessons of protest.' Rand Daily Mail, 5 February 1981, p11.
26 Mojapelo, JS. 'He forged an empire on the lessons of protest.' Rand Daily Mail, 5 February 1981, p11.
27 Edom M. Black Traders in US are tops, The Post, October 27, 1980, p5
28 Staff Reporter, 'Black Chain all set for growth.' Rand Daily Mail, June 27, 1979, p4
29 Kotlolo, M. Tribute to John Jack Lesolang, Sowetan, May 19, 1995, p7

# CONCLUSION

SJJ Lesolang was not merely an educator who transitioned into a businessman. He was a leader, a trailblazer, and a champion of progress for his community. His life was an embodiment of the courage to challenge the status quo, the determination to transform obstacles into opportunities, and the unwavering commitment to uplift others.

His story serves as an enduring beacon of inspiration for aspiring entrepreneurs and leaders, proving that with tenacity, vision, and a sense of purpose, one can indeed overcome the odds and leave a lasting impact on society. Lesolang's legacy thus serves as a powerful testament to the transformative power of education, entrepreneurship, and dedicated leadership.

# AN GADI

## A VISIONARY RETAILER AND INFLUENTIAL LANDLORD

Gadi family archives: AN Gadi

# HUMBLE BEGINNINGS TO AN INFLUENTIAL POSITION IN BUSINESS

Amos Nzimeni (AN) Gadi's rise from humble beginnings to an influential position in business is a testament to his visionary character. Born into a family of rural farm labourers, he managed to transition from a shop assistant to a retailer; director of a bank and landlord to several multinational companies.

Gadi was born on June 19, 1923, in Molteno, Eastern Cape province, to the Gcina and Xhamela clans.[1] His parents were both involved in farm work; his mother in the farmhouse and his father in the farm operations. Tragically, Gadi lost his father when he was only eight years old, after which his mother became a domestic servant in Molteno.

Despite his early hardships, Gadi persevered in his education until he passed Standard Six. He then moved on to find employment as a shop assistant at a Jewish family-owned general dealer. Like many young men in Molteno, he actively participated in community life; playing rugby, involving himself in church activities, and joining a social singing group called Merry Makers. He married Catherine Cele, and they were blessed with four daughters.[2]

[1] Author's interview with Linda Bosman (AN Gadi's daughter), August 5, 2023. Also see Government Gazette No.21788, December 1, 2000, p81
[2] Author's interview with Linda Bosman (AN Gadi's daughter), August 5, 2023

Gadi family archives: The Grosvenor General Dealer in Lusikisiki

Gadi's close relationship with his Jewish employers even led to his understanding of some Hebrew, as his daughter, Linda Bosman, fondly remembered.

"*Papa could speak a bit of the Jewish language,*" said Bosman, adding that Gadi felt a connection with his Jewish acquaintances.[3]

## GADI'S RETAIL JOURNEY: FROM SHOP ASSISTANT TO FRIENDSHIP WITH RAYMOND ACKERMAN

Gadi's quest for success led him from the general dealer in Molteno to Cape Town, where he sought greater opportunities, or "*greener pastures*", as it is often said. In Cape Town, Gadi found employment as a shop assistant with Ackermans.[4] The clothing retailer had been founded by Raymond Ackerman's father, Gus, and friends after World War I.[5]

3 Ibid
4 Ibid
5 Ackerman, R, Hearing Grasshoppers Jump, The Story of Raymond Ackerman as told to Denise Pritchard, p14-17

While working there, Gadi had the opportunity to study further and completed his matric through a night study programme that involved University of Cape Town (UCT) students. Bosman was told that it was during this time that Gadi met Raymond Ackerman. Raymond, as a student at UCT, was also connected to the night study programme.[6]

Ackerman's commitment to education is detailed in his book, *Hearing Grasshoppers Jump, The Story of Raymond Ackerman as told to Denise Prichard*. In the book, Ackerman describes his efforts, along with other students, to develop the first Student Health and Welfare Organisation Night Schools, even teaching at one of them.[7]

*"When he (Gadi) got to Ackermans, he was neat and eager to learn,"* recalled Bosman, adding her father became personal friends with (Raymond) Ackerman, who even visited Gadi in Lusikisiki.[8]

Gadi family archives: (Left) PG Gumede and (right) AN Gadi

While the 92-year-old Ackerman could not recall all the events in his earlier years, he remembered Gadi as follows:

*"I certainly remember Amos Gadi… and being impressed with him. He was a very good man."*[9]

After Ackermans, Gadi took up a position as clerk at an electrical company, Electricraft (Pty) Ltd. However, like many black people of his time, Gadi's movements were constrained by pass laws. If he wished to visit his family and home in Molteno, he had to ask his employers for employment confirmation and outline his travel plans.[11]

## FROM ELECTRICRAFT TO FISH AND CHIPS

It was while working at Electricraft that Gadi spotted an opportunity to venture into business. Drawing on his retail experience, he opened a fish and chips business named AMCA Fisheries; a name reflecting the first two letters of both his name and his wife Catherine's. At the time, Catherine was a qualified nurse.[12]

*"My mother had to stop working when they opened the shop. She was the one running the fish and chips shop,"* said Bosman.

6   Ibid
7   Ackerman, R, "Hearing Grasshoppers Jump, The Story of Raymond Ackerman as told to Denise Pritchard", p42
8   Author's interview with Linda Bosman (AN Gadi's daughter), August 5, 2023
9   Author's interview with Raymond Ackerman, August 7, 2023
10  Author's interview with Linda Bosman (AN Gadi's daughter), August 5, 2023
11  AN Gadi Family Archives, Letter from Registering Officer City of Cape Town Native Registration Department to Amos Gadi, December 15, 1954 and Confirmation of Employment Letter signed by JC Davenport, Director, Electricraft (Pty) Ltd, December 8, 1954
12  Author's interview with Linda Bosman (AN Gadi's daughter), August 5, 2023

The business operated from rented premises in Gugulethu in Native Yards (NY) 21. The fish was sourced from the docks and the potatoes from the markets where Gadi's brother-in-law, April Cele, worked. During the holidays, Gadi's daughter (Bosman), then a student at St Theresa's boarding school in Swaziland, would return to Cape Town and assist with duties at the shop, even scraping the fish. Bosman remembers AMCA Fisheries employing about six workers.[13]

*"There was no grill in those days. There was frying and pickling... Papa started another business [fish and chips]. He took a friend from Molteno to manage it. Then he had a third shop. He later opened AMCA General Dealers at NY 52 in the late 1960s,"* Bosman added.

Around that time, Gadi began to involve himself more with the National Federated Chamber of Commerce (NAFCOC), entrusting the business to the competent care of his wife, Mama Catherine. According to Bosman, her father had a keen desire to help others. When AMCA General Dealers was launched, the fish and chips business at NY 21 was transferred to their nephew, allowing Mama Catherine to focus on the general dealer enterprise. The general dealer sold an assortment of goods ranging from clothes and napkins to maize and paraffin.[14]

Bosman also recalls that Mama Catherine, while she was still active as a nurse, had taken courses in skills such as typing and bookkeeping. [15]

*"My father was running around going to meetings at the Chamber of Commerce. The business was left with this strong woman [Mama Catherine] to run. She was very stern,"* Bosman explained, emphasising her mother's crucial role in managing the day-to-day operations while her father was engaged in NAFCOC work, mobilising other businesses.

13 Ibid
14 Ibid
15 Ibid

# RELOCATING
# TO TRANSKEI

In the late 1960s, the apartheid regime sought to control the migration of black people to the urban areas by encouraging them to go back to the reserves and open up businesses there. This led to the crafting of legislation known as the Promotion of the Economic Development of Bantu Homelands Act 46 of 1968, designed to help homeland "heads of state" create Bantustan-specific corporations.[16]

In the Transkei and Ciskei homelands, the Xhosa Development Corporation emerged as a government initiative, focused on acquiring white-controlled trading stores and selling them to black traders. The white owners were compensated for their businesses and subsequently hired by the Xhosa Development Corporation as loan officers, responsible for training and monitoring the new black owners. This occurred during a period when rural trading stores in the Transkei were facing increased pressure.

Bus operators transported people from rural areas to the small towns, allowing them to find goods at cheaper prices, which in turn, affected the market for rural traders.[17]

Sensing an opportunity, the Gadi family decided to reinvest their capital in the Transkei. Bosman recalls a scheme organised by Transkei leader KD Matanzima to have black people take over white-controlled enterprises. By seizing the opportunities provided by government initiatives and legislation at the time, they managed to grow and adapt their business in the face of challenges, marking an inspiring chapter in the entrepreneurial journey of the Gadi family.

Now, Gadi had the task of convincing Mama Catherine about the potential advantages in the Transkei compared to Cape Town. It is said Gadi also encouraged other Cape Town-based entrepreneurs, such as S Zuma (affectionately known as "Boy"), to relocate to the Transkei.[18]

> *"It was a struggle... it is not easy to be uprooted from a place you are used to... Papa [Gadi] left first,"* said Bosman.

16  Brooks, P.E.J and Thomas, C.J. The Comparative and International Law Journal of Southern Africa, Vol 10 No. July 2, 1977, p141. Also See Ndzamela, P, BBBEE – Engineered at the Apartheid Workshop and Piloted under HF Verwoerd Irony of expecting turkey to vote for Christmas, Southern Centre for Inequality Studies, University of the Witwatersrand, September 2021.
17  Nkonyeni, A, "Black Property Pioneer", p43–46ss
18  Author's interview with Linda Bosman (AN Gadi's daughter), August 5, 2023
19  Ibid

Gadi family archives: (Far right) AN Gadi with his wife, (left) S Zuma and his wife

The Gadi family took their money from Cape Town and invested it in a business in the small Transkei town of Lusikisiki in the Mpondoland region.[19]

*"He [Gadi] started with a general dealer at Lusikisiki called Grosvenor General Dealer. It was a general dealer in the true sense... There were also sheep hides and building materials sold there,"* added Bosman.[20]

Grosvenor General Dealer later transformed into a SavMor (Spar brand). The brilliance of this transformation, according to Bosman, lay in Gadi's ability to source inventory for the store from Spar and pay later after selling the goods, without incurring interest charges.

Gadi also operated another general dealer business in another part of town, where he collaborated with Boy Zuma from NAFCOC.[21]

In 1973, when NAFCOC hosted its ninth annual conference in Mafeking, Zuma served as the convenor of the credentials ad hoc committee,[22] while Gadi was a member of the resolutions ad hoc committee. Gadi later ascended to the leadership of NAFCOC in the Transkei as President of the Transkei Chamber of Commerce, founded in 1972, while Zuma served as assistant secretary nationally.[23] NAFCOC's longest-serving President, Sam Motsuenyane, specifically acknowledged Gadi, alongside SJJ Lesolang and CDM Rabotho, as one of the many real leaders and champions *"who made great personal sacrifices to support the chamber".*[24]

In the late 1970s, Gadi diversified his interests by getting involved in property through a company called Zidlekhaya (Pty) Ltd, which acquired real estate from the Xhosa Development Corporation.[25]

[20]   Ibid
[21]   Ibid
[22]   UNISA Archives, ACC290, NAFCOC Minutes of the Ninth Annual Conference Held at Mafeking, May 17-20, 1973
[23]   UNISA Archives, ACC290, Transkei Chamber of Commerce Report, NAFCOC Tenth Annual Conference, Mthatha, June 20-23 1974
[24]   Hetherington I, Heroes of the Struggle, Interview with Dr S Motsuenyane, p128
[25]   Nkonyeni, A, "Black Property Pioneer", p115

*"The initiation of this project was the brainchild of a very enterprising businessman from Lusikisiki. His name was Amos Nzimeni Gadi and he was assisted by another committed and dependable operator from Mbizana by the name of Solomon Nchuka Jwacu. The property, on the periphery of Mthatha's central business district then, was bought. Because of its location, it was loosely referred to as the Madeira Street property,"* recalled property pioneer Archie Nkonyeni.[26]

The Madeira property faced challenges as a stand-alone business and struggled with full-time management. The chairman, Jwacu, was responsible for the supervision, but found it difficult as he ran his own business in Mbizana, about 200km from Mthatha. When Jwacu stepped down, Gadi also had a similar challenge as he was based in Lusikisiki. The reluctance to invest in full-blown property management, and concerns that a call for a hands-on management approach would have been interpreted as a lack of confidence in the leadership,[27] slowed the business's growth.

*"However, as time went on, members started making noises about what one of them once described as a semi-investment,"* said Nkonyeni.[28]

Eventually, Archie Nkonyeni, a resident of Mthatha, took on the role of an unpaid administrator, collecting rent. When another property came on the market, it was rebuilt as the Elliot Street Property with Ellerines as a tenant. Zidlekhaya then had two commercial properties, with the first property in Madeira Street being redeveloped and named "Mazwai Centre" after Professor Lizo Mazwai, who was the chairman of the group. The Elliot Street property was renamed **"Jwacu-Gadi Centre".** Later, at the dawn of democracy in the country, Zidlekhaya assets were transferred to a new larger venture, forming Modern Business Holdings (Pty) Ltd.[29]

In the 1980s, the retail business that had once been Grosvenor General Dealers and SavMor, was demolished as Gadi shifted from active operations into real estate, preparing for retirement. In its place, he built a complex called AMCA Centre, renting spaces to various tenants, including KFC, optometrists and hairdressers.[30]

Bosman reminisces about her father starting another general dealer in downtown Lusikisiki, later partnering with Brown's Cash & Carry, now under the Massmart stable. In this deal, Gadi was the landlord, owning the property and sharing in the retail operations.[31] A 2022 Massmart Broad-Based Black Economic Empowerment Certificate showed that Brown's Cash & Carry in Lusikisiki traded as Gadi's Cash & Carry, with a business registration number dating back to 1988.[32]

26  Ibid
27  Ibid
28  Ibid, p116.
29  Ibid, p117-121s
30  Author's interview with Linda Bosman (AN Gadi's daughter), August 5, 2023
31  Ibid
32  Massmart Broad-Based Black Economic Empowerment, https://www.massmart.co.za/wp-content/uploads/2022/10/Massmart_HR_GEN_2740_22_Annexure.pdf

# VENTURES IN TIMBER, BRICKMAKING & AGRICULTURE

Gadi saw an opportunity to acquire land in the densely forested areas in Lusikisiki. Upon obtaining the wooded area, he started a sawmill, making coffins, tables and other timber products. One of Gadi's mottos, as recounted by Bosman, was:

*"bietjie bietjie maak meer",* meaning "little by little can make more".

Following the sale of the wood, Gadi's entrepreneurial spirit led him to turn the land into a farm, producing chickens and eggs, potatoes, oranges, bananas, and even tobacco. Although he initially hired a manager for the farm, it didn't work out as envisaged; but to this day, the farmland remains active and the family continues to cultivate it.[33]

Gadi's agricultural interests extended beyond his own farm. He served as a director of Lambasi Farms (Pty) Ltd, a maize-growing initiative in Lambasi in the Transkei region.[34]

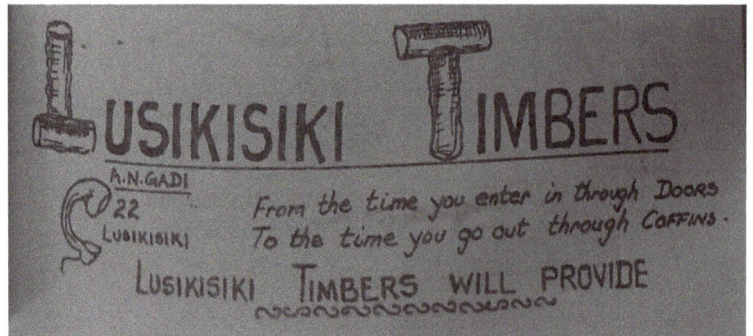

UNISA Archives, Nafcoc Papers: Advert of AN Gadi's timber business

In a move to meet the local housing demands, Gadi also started Gadi Brickyard in Lusikisiki at a time when many people were still using mud to build their homes. He brought in skilled brickmakers from Molteno and ingeniously sourced the coal for the manufacturing of the bricks from a nearby hospital and prison. However, when those two institutions stopped using coal, the brickyard faced a significant challenge. Unfortunately, the management of the brickyard failed to innovate, leading to the closure of the business.[35]

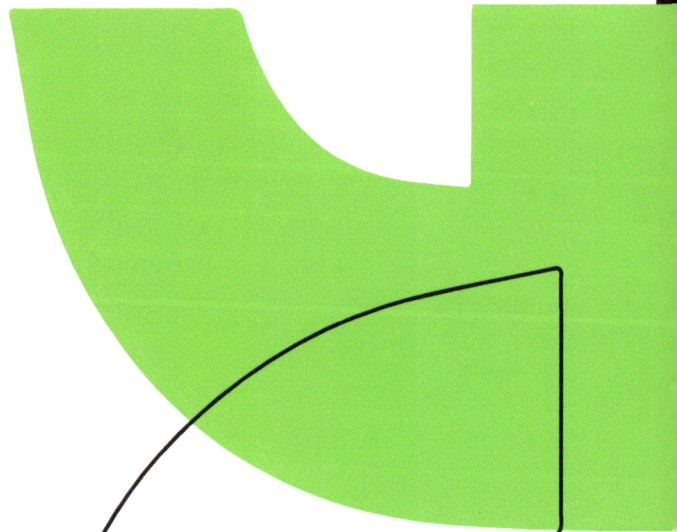

Gadi family archives: (Far right) in dark suit; AN Gadi

33 Author's interview with Linda Bosman (AN Gadi's daughter), August 5, 2023
34 Nkonyeni, A, Black Property Pioneer, p140
35 Author's interview with Linda Bosman (AN Gadi's daughter), August 5, 2023

# BECOMING A FOUNDING DIRECTOR OF AFRICAN BANK

Gadi played a crucial role in realising the vision for African Bank, ochestrating a campaign, with other leaders, to raise R1 million. With his persistent door-to-door fundraising efforts in Lusikisiki and organising innovative events such as beauty concerts, Gadi successfully garnered investment.

His trustworthy reputation in the community made many people willing to invest in African Bank. Bosman recalled that he worked with *"Tat' Jwacu"* (Solomon Jwacu),[36] and his relentless efforts culminated in his being among the founding directors and shareholders of African Bank in May 1975.[37]

After years of dedicated service to the business world, Gadi began to wind down and retired from active business in 1987. Recognising his significant contribution, NAFCOC honoured him by hosting a two-day function at the Wild Coast Sun Hotel in the Transkei. On the programme of speakers were Boy Zuma, Sam Motsuenyane, Archie Nkoyeni as Master of Ceremonies, and Wiseman Nkuhlu, who gave the vote of thanks.[38]

# CONCLUSION

Gadi passed away in September 1995. In his lifetime he had travelled the world to the US, UK and China.[39] Almost six decades after Gadi's businesses took shape, his business legacy continues to thrive, particularly in the property sector. However, some legal disputes remained unsettled, threatening the stability of some of his assets.[40] Gadi's story stands as an inspiring testament to tenacity, trust, and entrepreneurial spirit, leaving an indelible mark on African business history. His role in African Bank's founding and his enduring impact on the community, celebrate the spirit of innovation and resilience. He is not just remembered for his commercial success, but is also celebrated for his significant contributions to his community and the broader economy. His legacy continues to inspire, underscoring the timeless relevance of his approach to business and life.

36  Ibid
37  NATIONAL ARCHIVES OF SOUTH AFRICA, RB160, Particulars of Subscriber, May 30, 1975
38  AN Gadi Family Archives, Function in Recognition of Mr AN Gadi's Contribution to Nafcoc as he retires, November 6-7, 1987
39  Author's interview with Linda Bosman (AN Gadi's daughter), August 5, 2023
40  Mfazwe v AN Gadi Property Investments (Pty) Ltd (CA192/2014) [2015] ZAECGHC 24 (7 April 2015)

# Richard *Maponya*

Bailey's African History Archive: Richard Maponya

The determined entrepreneur who built a lasting empire against all odds

# *After seven decades in commerce,* Richard Maponya's name remains synonymous with business success.

Richard Maponya had conceived the idea of becoming a clothing retailer in Soweto as early as the 1950s, but racist legislation hindered that vision as black people were restricted from participating in the fashion business. When he was denied a licence to sell clothes in the 1950s, he started the Dube Hygienic Dairy and provided a bicycle delivery service to customers without electricity and refrigerators.[1]

The dairy sector was not unfamiliar to Maponya, as he had grown up milking cattle in his home village when he was young.[2]

Born in 1920 in the village of Lenyenye, Limpopo, Maponya initially trained to be a teacher but found a job at a clothing company. His manager offered him some garments that he could sell in his spare time. However, when he wanted to start his own business, the discriminatory laws were stacked against him.[3]

## Undeterred, he turned to what he knew best.

But starting up was not easy. He needed cash to establish the dairy business, and banks were reluctant to provide the required capital. It is said that Maponya found a contractor willing to build the dairy on favourable terms. He then invested his savings in the dairy business, offering milk to thousands of people in Soweto.[4]

Maponya employed 20 men on bicycles for deliveries, and within four years, the business had created more jobs with the delivery staff growing to 100. The annual turnover of the milk business reportedly grew from R100 000 to R800 000. Maponya's wife, Marina, was very instrumental in helping the business to grow.[5]

Bailey's African History Archive: Richard Maponya and his wife, Marina Maponya

1   Ndzamela P, Native Merchants, The Building of the Black Business Class in South Africa, p154
2   Mtshali, L, "Maponya says mall is highlight of long career", Business Times, November 9, 2008, p4
3   Ndzamela P, Native Merchants, The Building of the Black Business Class in South Africa, p153-154
4   Holmes, M, "Soweto's first milk man now owns a mint", The Sunday Star, Sunday Profile, October 21, 1984, p6
5   Mandy, N, A City Divided, Johannesburg and Soweto, p267

When profits started declining in the milk business, the Maponyas sold it and redirected the capital towards building a shopping centre, Maponya's Supply Stores.[6]

Later the Maponyas expanded their business empire to include a variety of ventures such as a butchery, grocery store, restaurant, bottle stores, fuel stations and a motor dealership.[7]

*As a successful businessman, other merchants in Johannesburg looked up to him as a leader.*

In the inaugural conference of the National African Federated Chamber of Commerce (NAFCOC), Maponya was elected as the first president of the organisation. Maponya had been the chairman of the Johannesburg African Chamber of Commerce established in 1955. The objective of the organisation was to unite business people on the Witwatersrand. However, over time, they felt it was important to unite black business people through a national organisation.[8]

Maponya saw business associations like NAFCOC as enablers of unity and commercial strength among black African entrepreneurs.

*"We must have associations for the same reasons that other businesspeople everywhere in the world have thought it wise to have them. They are a means of Unity, without which the African Trader remains a weakling unable to withstand the rigorous challenge and acute competition coming from outside his areas,"* Maponya wrote in NAFCOC's African Trader magazine in the first quarter of 1967.[9]

*"Nor is there any chance or hope that we can learn and improve our businesses to the extent that we may enjoy an ever-increasing patronage from our own people, without first working together as businessmen."[10]*

Way back in the 1960s, Maponya knew that leveraging supply chain networks and pricing goods well, played a big role in the battle for the customer. Maponya would note that the small African businessman found it difficult to charge the same low prices as the supermarkets and bazaars in downtown Johannesburg, because the African business people bought their stock in small quantities at inflated prices and could not benefit from discounts allowed on

Financial Mail, "Marina Maponya, Petticoat tycoon", September 3, 1982
Ndzamela P, Native Merchants, The Building of the Black Business Class in South Africa, p134
Motsuenyane, S, A Testament of Hope, The Autobiography of Sam Motsuenyane, p61-63
Maponya, R.P, The African Trader, "The Need For Unity Among Traders", January-March 1967, p16
Ibid

bulk purchases. These market dynamics, Maponya believed, cost the African entrepreneur not only a loss of income but also customer confidence. Maponya was frank enough to understand that Africans could not be forced to buy from his fellow African merchant, if prices were not competitive and service was absent.[11]

*Although he did not serve for a long time as NAFCOC president, Maponya took a lead in business operations. His commercial life outlived many of his peers, and his name continues to be well-known in the business world, seven decades after he started out as an entrepreneur.*

In addition to his involvement in the chamber of commerce, Maponya was also active in politics through his Lebowa National Party. He campaigned to be part of the Urban Bantu Council in Soweto.[12]

Despite his success as a businessman and his relative wealth, Maponya's money did not buy him immunity from racism. In January 1977, while driving from the Turffontein racecourse, a white motorist known as Frederick Johan Louwrens, is said to have accosted Maponya and told him "Kaffir, don't drive as if you're in Soweto". Maponya would later tell the Johannesburg Magistrate Court that Louwrens threatened to kill him and had waved his gun at him. As a man of high standing, Maponya felt humiliated and took the matter up.[13]

Maponya was a registered racehorse owner; a sport typically associated with wealthy people.[14]

In 1980, the Maponyas became the first black entrepreneurs to be awarded a motor franchise by General Motors. They were allowed to sell new and used cars in Soweto.[15] Known as Mountain Motors, the General Motors dealership was operated by Richard and Marina Maponya. They sold Opel, Chevrolet and Isuzu vehicles.[16]

Maponya's business career was highly decorated. In 2007, President Thabo Mbeki, awarded him the Order of the Baobab in Silver, alongside Sally Motlana. Maponya was recognised for his inspiration to disadvantaged South Africans and his contribution to entrepreneurship under oppressive apartheid conditions.[17]

The highlight of Maponya's entrepreneurial career was the opening of the Maponya Mall in Soweto in 2007. He had identified the land decades earlier but had been denied ownership. It was only after South Africa transitioned to democracy that he was allowed to buy the land. He approached banks for funding, and they advised him to form a consortium as the project was too big. Maponya partnered with Zenprop Property Holdings, and they were funded by Investec to build the Mall.[18]

The Mall has arguably immortalised the Maponya name for decades to come.

## The businessman passed away in January 2020 at the age of 99.[19]

11    Ibid, p16-17
12    Staff Reporter, Rand Daily Mail, "Maponya aims at UBC", August 5, 1967, p3
13    Staff Reporter, "Maponya tells of 'kaffir' jibe", Rand Daily Mail, September 21, 1977, p1
14    Mandy, N, A City Divided, Johannesburg and Soweto, p268
15    Mojapelo, JS, Rand Daily Mail, "Motor trade first for Soweto businessman", October 16, 1980, p11
16    Rand Daily Mail advert, January 23, 1981, p20
17    Richard John Pelwana Maponya, Order of Baobab, Silver, https://www.thepresidency.gov.za/richard-john-pelwana-maponya-1926
18    Mtshali, L, "Maponya says mall is highlight of long career", Business Times, November 9, 2008, p4
19    President Cyril Ramaphosa on the passing of Dr Richard Maponya, https://www.gov.za/news/media-statements/president-cyril-ramaphosa-passing-dr-richard-maponya-06-jan-2020

# HM PITJE

## THE EMBODIMENT OF BLACK CONSCIOUSNESS OF BUSINESS

*From domestic servant to pioneer in visual media and founding shareholder of African Bank*

During the dark days of apartheid, Hezekiah Mothibe "HM" Pitje emerged as a beacon of hope, running a cinema business in Mamelodi, a township in Pretoria, where he beamed movies to crowds of black African audiences in search of much-needed alternative entertainment. This was before the advent of television in South Africa in 1976, and a period when many black African business people were primarily involved in trading and shopkeeping.

Pitje is said to have begun his cinematic journey by projecting movies in a garage before progressing to a larger space, and eventually establishing a cinema famously known as Thebu Cinema in Mamelodi.

HM Pitje family archives: Hezekiah Mothibe "HM" Pitje

THEBU CINEMA

Cor. Tsweu & Mashabela Streets,
P.O. BOX 1,
MAMELODI,
PRETORIA.
Phone: 8 Mamelodi

Telegraphic address:-
"MATHEBULE"

PROPRIETOR: H. M. PITJE

National Archives of South Africa: TPD, 3065/1969

Thebu Cinema, inaugurated in 1964, stood as a testament to Pitje's fortitude. This was during a time when it was a struggle for black people to acquire the necessary trading licences and such concessions were seldom granted to them. Nevertheless, he persevered, confronting the authorities until they eventually granted him permission to operate his cinema business. Pitje's widow, Vuyelwa Alice Pitje (Mme Pitje), recalled that the name of the cinema **"Thebu"**, was derived from "Mathebula", Pitje's mother, and was a tribute to her.[1]

Thebu Cinema operated on Corner Tsewu and Mashabela Streets with the address: P.O. Box 1, Mamelodi, Pretoria. Its telegraphic address was "Mathebule". The cinema's annual financial statements for the year ended February 28, 1965, showed the company had a balance sheet of R12 115.66c, as verified by the chartered accountants, Von Gesau, Kurtzahn & Thompson.[2]

## But how did HM Pitje's remarkable journey begin?

His life started during the dramatic years of World War I. Pitje was born on September 7, 1914, in Phokwane, Sekhukhune district, in the present-day Limpopo Province of South Africa. As a young boy, Pitje spent his early years looking after his blind grandfather and, as a result, he only started formal education when he was ten years old, according to Mme Pitje.[4]

*"In 1931, he got his Standard Six (certificate) but could not go further because they (his family) were so poor; they had nothing. He decided with a friend that they should go to Pretoria. They hitchhiked and went via Middelburg to meet an uncle, who gave them money to get to Pretoria. From there he looked for work and the only work he could secure was domestic work,"* Mme Pitje recounted.[5]

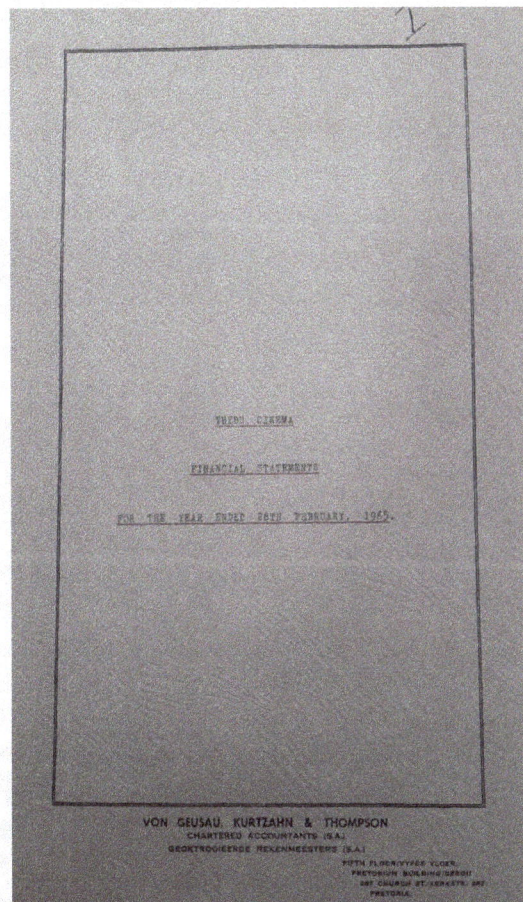

National Archives of South Africa: TPD, 3065/1969

[1]   Author's interview with Mrs Vuyelwa Alice Pitje, June 16, 2023
[2]   National Archives of South Africa, TPD, 3065/1969, Illiquid Case Payment. In the Supreme Court of South Africa, Transvaal Provincial Division, Hezekiah Mothibe Pitje versus Gallo Africa Limited
[3]   National Archives of South Africa, BAO, Vol 3879, C100/6/6607, Application for a South African Passport, HM Pitje, April 28, 1972
[4]   Author's interview with Mrs Vuyelwa Alice Pitje, June 16, 2023
[5]   Ibid

In Pretoria, Pitje initially worked for an Afrikaans-speaking family, but a significant language barrier and his poor comprehension of Afrikaans led to his hasty departure. The story goes that the lady of the Afrikaans-speaking household had given HM Pitje an instruction along the lines of *"Pikinin, jy moet 'n vuur aansteek (Child, you must start a fire)".* But he could not understand the instruction and went to sit on a chair in the kitchen instead of starting a fire, much to his employer's annoyance. His inability to follow the command resulted in a swift dismissal!

Undeterred, Pitje then looked for another job as a domestic worker and found one with an English-speaking family, who were apparently much nicer to him.[6]

*"While he was working there, he sought their permission to host a film screening as he owned a 16mm projector. The family was generous enough to let him show films to domestic workers from the surrounding areas, for which he charged them a tickey at the time,"* recalled Mme Pitje.

A *"tickey"* was a South African three-penny coin that is now no longer in circulation. Mme Pitje believes these modest *"tickey"* film shows could be seen as the humble beginnings of Pitje's entrepreneurial journey. The employer's garage was the bioscope where the films were screened; attended by fellow domestic workers from the area, captivated by the moving pictures on the wall.

Always seeking to improve his lot and ambitious to do better in life, Pitje later spotted a job advert of the HF Verwoerd Hospital, now known as Steve Biko Academic Hospital. The healthcare facility was hiring orderlies, and he applied and secured the job. It was during this time at the hospital that the idea of his second business venture came about. During his tenure at HF Verwoerd Hospital, he managed to save enough money to purchase a camera that he used to take photos to supplement his income. This venture eventually evolved into a café in Mamelodi. Mme Pitje says these businesses were established before their relationship, as both had previously been married and lost their spouses.[7] Pitje was initially married to Mammotsa Marakgadi Salome Pitje, who predeceased her husband in 1975.[8]

Court records from the 1960s described Pitje as an operator of a general dealer, fresh produce business and cinema.[9]

The establishment of Thebu Cinema in 1964 and the challenges Pitje faced in the process, as recounted by Mme Pitje, are also documented in a newspaper article in the *Post*, dated March 1, 1979.

6  Ibid
7  Ibid
8  Staff Reporter, Rand Daily Mail, Mrs Pitje buried, Monday September 15, 1975, p1
9  National Archives of South Africa, TPD, 3065/1969, Illiquid Case Payment, In the Supreme Court of South Africa, Transvaal Provincial Division, Hezekiah Mothibe Pitje versus Gallo Africa Limited

The article, headlined *"Restrictions on Traders Attacked",* stated that Pitje initially leased the cinema business for 10 years before buying it from the Central Transvaal Administration Board. The article lauded Pitje as the most successful black pioneer in the cinema business. He was described as having opened the Thebu Cinema during a period when black people were legally barred from owning such establishments in urban areas. The *Post* would quote Moses Maubane, an executive director of NAFCOC and later African Bank director, who described Pitje as a courageous man who *"was able to persuade the authorities to grant him a licence in what was and still is a rare business among the black people".*[10]

The *Post* further wrote that Pitje had faced scepticism from his own black community, many of whom preferred cinemas run by Indian operators in Marabastad, which were perceived as superior. Yet, Pitje worked to challenge these stereotypes and tried to convince NAFCOC to establish a national film company operating across all black townships.[11]

The role of Indian families in the cinema business is noteworthy. Prominent among these was AB Moosa, who along with AI Kajee, opened the Avalon Theatre in Durban in 1939.[12] In Johannesburg's Soweto township, the well-known businessman Ephraim Tshabalala "ET", owned the Eyethu Cinema built in 1968.[13]

In addition to managing the Thebu Cinema in Mamelodi, Pitje also operated a mobile cinema business that screened movies at various locations in Ga-Rankuwa. However, the operation was not always smooth-sailing. At one point in Ga-Rankuwa, his screenings were disrupted because he could not procure lamps for his projectors; a supply chain issue with his service provider.[14]

Pitje's involvement in the visual media business extended beyond the Transvaal as he held a directorship in the Rio Cinema in the township of New Brighton in Port Elizabeth.[15] His movie house featured international drama films like *Echoes of a Summer, Churchill's Leopards* and martial arts film *Secret Rivals.*[16] He also had local content, which featured Sam Mhangwani's *The Unfaithful* and *The Ken Gampu Show.*[17]

Pitje used more than just traditional advertising through newspapers and posters to promote his shows. He implemented other strategic methods to drive traffic to his cinema. These measures included a bus service that picked up customers near their homes and transported them to the cinema in Mamelodi. In January 1967, Pitje would claim in court documents that his cinema lost just over R400 in the period between June 27 and September 12, 1966, alleging that the bus repairer had failed to adequately fix the vehicle.[18]

National Archives of South Africa: TPD, 3065/1969

[9] Independent Newspapers, Post, Restrictions on Traders Attacked, March 1, 1979, p7.
[10] Independent Newspapers, Post, Restrictions on Traders Attacked, March 1, 1979, p7.
[11] Calpin, CH, AI Kajee, His work for the Southern African Indian Community in South Africa History Online, https://www.sahistory.org.za/archive-ai-kajee-his-work-southern-african-indian-community-chapter-8
[12] Nzimande, P, Native Merchants, The Building of the Black Business Class, p138.
[13] Staff Reporter, Rand Daily Mail, Mr. Pitje needs lamps, Wednesday, March 1, 1972.
[14] Mojapelo, J, Rand Daily Mail, Pitje windfall to servant, schools, Tuesday, October 1, 1954.
[15] Rand Daily Mail, Saturday, April 29, 1978, p5 and Tuesday, January 23, 1977, p2.
[16] Rand Daily Mail, Saturday, October 22, 1966, p3.
[17] National Archives of South Africa, TPD, 2256-1966, Illiquid Case Money Due, Meter Motors (Pty) Ltd versus HM Pitje, 1966.

Pitje was also a well-travelled and esteemed man. For instance, a passport application in 1972, showed that he requested travel documentation to visit Germany, Italy and England on vacation.[19] In a letter supporting his passport application, Pitje was described as a prominent resident of the Bantu township of Mamelodi, where he had various business interests.[20]

Another motivation from attorneys De Klerk & Kruger characterised Pitje as:

*"a man of high honour and one who has always been willing and able to meet his obligations even under difficult circumstances".[21]*

They described him as a man of high social standing amongst the Bantu people, not only in Mamelodi but throughout the country, who had earned the confidence of the government. The lawyers further noted that Pitje was also the mayor of the Mamelodi Bantu Township and served on the Advisory Committee of the City Council of Pretoria in Mamelodi township, where he operated a cinema and public entertainment business.[22]

Despite being well-regarded, Pitje was not afraid to voice objections to matters he disagreed with in judicial courts, the media and conferences.

He was firmly against white people owning shares in businesses established by black people and opposed the participation of white-controlled enterprises in the townships reserved for black people.

*"We have always been told that whites would come with their money and expertise. But I don't think we need it at all. We have got our own people with the necessary expertise and money and therefore we reject the idea which is only interested in exploiting blacks for the benefit of whites... As it is we are going to establish a finance corporation that will have more than R200 000, which will be needed in assisting those black businessmen who need financial assistance," argued Pitje.*

As a well-travelled man, Pitje was said to have been impressed by the economic independence of the black American entrepreneurs in the US.[23] He even withdrew from African Bank because of white shareholding.

19. National Archives of South Africa, BAO, Vol 3879, C100/6/6607, Application for a South African Passport, HM Pitje, April 28, 1972
20. Ibid, BAO, Vol 3879, C100/6/6607, Application for a South African Passport, HM Pitje, Letter from the Evangelical Lutheran Church, Transvaal Region, April 17, 1972
21. Ibid, BAO, Vol 3879, C100/6/6607, Application for a South African Passport, HM Pitje, Letter from the Evangelical Lutheran Church, Transvaal Region, April 17, 1972
22. Ibid, BAO, Vol 3879, C100/6/6607, Application for a South African Passport, HM Pitje, Letter of motivation from De Klerk & Kruger, April 12, 1972
23. Mashumi, V, Rand Daily Mail Pretoria Bureau, Mamelodi traders talk on partnership, Wednesday, October 3, 1979, p6

## PITJE'S CONTROVERSIAL WITHDRAWAL FROM AFRICAN BANK AND CONSTRUCTION VENTURE _____

The first edition of the *Rand Daily Mail* on September 1, 1977, featured a headline titled *"Whites in black bank rile Pitje"*. The newspaper reported that Pitje, the owner of a cinema in Mamelodi and executive member of NAFCOC, had withdrawn his support for the African Bank and demanded the immediate sale of his shares. The newspaper report stated that Pitje's objection stemmed from his strong belief that black people could run the African Bank without the participation of white shareholders.[24]

Upset by his statement in the press, NAFCOC retorted with a press statement, stating:

*"Mr Pitje's mysterious withdrawal of shares from the African Bank only exposes his insincerity and lack of commitment in so far as our NAFCOC projects are concerned. He had ample time to air his views at Executive meetings and at the NAFCOC Conference or even at the Bank's Annual General Meeting early this year. All shareholders of the Bank know that we do not expect the Bank to be profitable within the first or second year as much of the Bank's funds must be devoted to growth and the establishment of branches all over the Republic."[25]*

The statement further emphasised that African Bank was committed to employing blacks in high executive roles, based solely on merit, not race. It also denied making a particular statement attributed to the NAFCOC leadership and explained Pitje's dissatisfaction with African Bank as stemming from his failure to become a Director on the Board. The press statement also warned that Pitje's publicising of his grievances could create disunity when unity was needed.

Pitje's issue with white ownership in African Bank was not an isolated instance. He also boycotted a joint venture between NAFCOC and construction firm Murray & Roberts. Pitje withdrew his R2 000 contribution towards the formation of the initiative, arguing that *"blacks can do this without whites coming in as shareholders, whether as minority shareholders or not"*.

His belief was that white people should participate by sharing their expertise.[26]

24  Rand Daily Mail, Whites in black Bank rile Pitje", Thursday, September 1, 1977, p1-2
25  UNISA Archives, ACC290, NAFCOC Press Statement, September 1, 1977
26  Mojapelo, JS, Rand Daily Mail, NAFCOC executive pulls out, Tuesday, August, 1977 3, p1

Mme Pitje fondly recalls that back in the day, Pitje would offer advice to black petrol attendants at fuel garages, encouraging them to master their trade before venturing out to establish their own service station businesses.

*"That was what he wanted for black people. That is why in Mamelodi even for the underprivileged black children, he established a bursary fund. He helped a lot of people in Mamelodi, who became lawyers, doctors and teachers,"* Mme Pitje remembered.[27]

THEBU CINEMA
BALANCE SHEET AS AT 28TH FEBRUARY, 1965.

| CAPITAL ACCOUNT | | | | | |
|---|---|---|---|---|---|
| EXCESS INCOME FOR THE YEAR | 1,172 | 46 | | 408 | 46 |
| Less: Drawings | 764 | 00 | | | |
| | | | | | |
| LOAN ACCOUNTS | | | | | |
| AFRICAN CONSOLIDATED FILMS | 5,382 | 00 | | 11,707 | 20 |
| TRADE SERVICES | 842 | 69 | | | |
| NATIONAL INDUSTRIAL CREDIT CORPORATION - Motor Vehicle Account | 2,285 | 68 | | | |
| NATIONAL INDUSTRIAL CREDIT CORPORATION - Furniture and Fittings Account | 1,108 | 58 | | | |
| VOLKSKAS BEPERK | 2,088 | 25 | | | |

| FIXED ASSETS | | | | |
|---|---|---|---|---|
| PROJECTION MACHINERY AND EQUIPMENT | 7,370.00 | | | |
| Less: Depreciation | 1,843.00 | | 5,527 | 00 |
| FURNITURE AND FITTINGS | 1,991.84 | | | |
| Less: Depreciation | 199.84 | | 1,792 | 00 |
| MOTOR VEHICLES | 3,186.50 | | | |
| Less: Depreciation | 637.50 | | 2,549 | 00 |
| CURRENT ASSETS | | | | |
| THEBU KIOSK - Loan Account | | | 744 | 58 |
| AFRIKAHUS - Loan Account | | | 1,275 | 20 |
| JACK MALALEKU - Loan Account | | | 40 | 00 |
| ELECTRICITY DEPOSIT | | | 60 | 00 |
| TELEPHONE DEPOSIT | | | 20 | 00 |
| DEPOSIT ON TICKETS | | | 110 | 00 |

12,115 66

WE HAVE PREPARED THE BALANCE SHEET SET OUT ABOVE FROM THE BOOKS OF THEBU CINEMA.

VON GRÜNAU, KURTZAHN & THOMPSON

Per:

CHARTERED ACCOUNTANTS (S.A.)
AUDITORS

PRETORIA.
28th June, 1966.

National Archives of South Africa: TPD, 3065/1969

27  Author's interview with Mrs Vuyelwa Alice Pitje, June 16, 2023
28  Mojapelo, J, Rand Daily Mail, Pitje windfall to servant, schools, October 1, 1974, p1
29  Author's interview with Mrs Vuyelwa Alice Pitje, June 16, 2023

# ECONOMIC EMPOWERMENT

On his 60th birthday in 1974, Pitje launched the "HM Pitje Bursary Fund" with an initial donation of R1 000. Those who celebrated with him contributed an additional R85 to the fund. On the same day, he also reportedly presented R1 000 to John Mokoena, an employee who had worked for him as a driver for 27 years. The bursary fund committee consisted of Mr P Monoa, Rev TK Pomane, Mrs ET Sekati, Mr G Ntlatleng, Mr J Tau, Mr S Motebe and Mr S Kutumela.[28]

*"He always put himself behind... He was generous and he would not want to see other people suffering,"* said Mme Pitje recollecting that the giving nature of her husband was one of her fondest memories of him.[29]

She also remembered how Pitje championed the property rights of widows in Mamelodi and promoted sports in the township. It was for the role he played in sports development in black communities that the HM Pitje Stadium was named after him.

Pitje was credited as one of the sponsors of the local football association in Mamelodi, reportedly donating R1 000 annually. Local soccer teams used to compete for the *"Pitje Trophy",* which came with a R600 cash prize. This competition later evolved to the *"Pitje League",* featuring 32 teams from Mamelodi East and West.[30]

When the discussion about introducing a black television service took place in the late 1970s, Pitje suggested that the millions of rands budgeted for that should instead be used to address the housing shortages affecting thousands of people. Pitje questioned:

*" Of what value is TV to blacks at this time when most of us are hit by this housing shortage? "*[31]

However, HM Pitje's stances weren't always popular, Mme Pitje explained. As a municipal Councillor in Mamelodi, he faced opposition from his peers, with some threatening to *"bury him alive"*. His health began to deteriorate, leading to his resignation from the Council. The 1980s proved to be particularly challenging for the Pitje family. They faced a rates and taxes bill challenge from the Council and were asked to pay a significant sum which they believed to be excessive. Mme Pitje recounted that Pitje offered to pay the Council R10 000 a month, but the proposal was apparently rejected. The Pitje family later learnt of a political war being waged against them by opponents.

30  Rand Daily Mail, Councillor's plea on Pitje stadium, Tuesday September 8, 1981, p18, and Veleleni, M, Rand Daily Mail, Pitje Boosts Soccer, August 5, 1977, p10
31  Post, Use TV Money For Housing Says Pitje, Jan 15, 1979, p6

# legacy

The matter ended up in court and led to Pitje's sequestration. Fortunately, because they were married out of community of property, their home was saved. A commission of inquiry tried to address the unfairness, according to Mme Pitje, but the efforts did not yield any significant results.[32]

*"We persevered until we could no longer fight,"* reflected Mme Pitje.[33]

During the prosperous times, Pitje had wanted his wife to devote her time to nurturing their children at home. However, as Pitje aged, Mme Pitje began to play a more active role in the business, doing stock taking, supervising workers and solving problems. Mme Pitje was well-equipped for this role, holding qualifications as a professional midwife and a BCare degree with honours. In the 1980s, she started selling cosmetics and cleaning detergents. She had come from a family of entrepreneurs and at a young age used to help behind the family shop counter. After 1989, she became the primary breadwinner in the family. Returning to her roots in nursing, she also sold Tupperware and clothing at the hospital. The family home was still under a mortgage, but they managed to make ends meet while raising school-aged children.[34]

Pitje died in August 1997 at the age of 83. His funeral service was held at the stadium that bore his name; the HM Pitje Stadium. He left behind an impressive legacy as a businessman, community builder, and the inaugural mayor of Mamelodi.[35]

[32] Author's interview with Mrs Vuyelwa Alice Pitje, June 16 2023
[33] Author's interview with Mrs Vuyelwa Alice Pitje, June 16 2023
[34] Author's interview with Mrs Vuyelwa Alice Pitje, June 16 2023
[35] Mothibeli, T, The Star, First Mamelodi Mayor to be Buried Today, August 21, 1997, p6

# CONCLUSION

HM Pitje was a beacon of black empowerment, who epitomised the spirit of self-determination and entrepreneurship. Rising from humble beginnings, he harnessed his business acumen to build a flourishing empire, navigating his way through complex socio-economic landscapes with unparalleled resilience. His steadfast conviction in the potential of black-owned businesses and his unwavering stand against white ownership in black-established entities, cemented his place in history as a pioneering force in the face of apartheid-era restrictions.

Beyond his business ventures, Pitje's commitment to his community was an equally compelling aspect of his legacy. His initiatives in education, healthcare, and local sports demonstrated his deep-seated belief in uplifting those around him. His wife, Mme Pitje, who stood beside him in every endeavour, carried on his legacy, displaying similar resilience and entrepreneurial spirit during challenging times.

Pitje's journey was not without hardship, but his tenacity and commitment to black empowerment remained undeterred, making him a true embodiment of the Black Consciousness of Business. His life serves as an inspiring testament to the power of self-belief, determination, and unwavering commitment to community and equality, resonating with and inspiring future generations to champion the same values. The story of Pitje is, therefore, not merely a narrative of individual accomplishment, but a testament to the enduring spirit of community upliftment and black entrepreneurship in apartheid-era South Africa.

# THE IMPACT OF THE GROUP AREAS ACT ON BLACK ENTREPRENEURS

## FROM HUMBLE BEGINNINGS

### THE STORY OF PK SEABELA

From humble beginnings in a role demeaningly termed *"kitchen boy"*, Petrus Maphoko (PK) Seabela rose to become the owner of a successful printing business, Victory Press, located in Johannesburg's central business district. However, in the 1950s, the discriminatory Group Areas Act forced him to vacate his business premises, as the law had designated the location as a *"white area".*[1]

Born in 1905 in Pietersburg, Northern Transvaal (now Limpopo Province), Seabela married Ntebatse Motsi.

Mweli Skota, a journalist, businessman, and former secretary-general of the African National Congress, described Seabela as an ambitious man who was constantly seeking to enhance his knowledge and financial standing. Yet, the Group Areas Act frustrated his efforts, compelling him to relocate Victory Press from Main Street in downtown Johannesburg to the township of Orlando.[2] The Group Areas Act No.41 of 1950 was a racially motivated law aimed at controlling land occupation, premise use, and the acquisition of immovable property along racial lines. The segmentation was done both for residential and business purposes.[3]

P. K. SEABELA

Wits Historical Papers Research Archive, Skota Papers

National Archives of South Africa: KJB, N1/4/3-1601/75

Arriving in Johannesburg in the 1920s, Seabela initially worked in a kitchen before securing employment at the Central News Agency (CNA). It was while working at the *Daily Express* newspaper that he conceived the idea of owning a printing press.

In 1946, he purchased Victory Press from its owners, employing about 17 African workers.[4] In 1957, Seabela and fellow businessman William Davies (described as coloured) were fined for operating a business from premises in an area designated for whites only.

1   Wits Historical Papers Research Archive, Bantu World newspaper, 1935-1955, From kitchen boy to head of firm---- now he has to move, 24 December 1955, p2
2   Wits Historical Papers Research Archive, Skota Papers A1618, p29
3   See Group Areas Act, https://blogs.loc.gov/law/files/2014/01/Group-Areas-Act-1950.pdf
4   Wits Historical Papers Research Archive, Bantu World newspaper, 1935-1955, From kitchen boy to head of firm---- now he has to move, 24 December 1955, p2

An article on PK Seabela in the *Bantu World* newspaper in December 1955

**From kitchen boy to head of firm -- now he has to move**

P. K. Seabela, proprietor of the Victory Press in Main Street, Johannesburg, one of the traders who has received notice to quit. Mr. Seabela has a huge printing plant in his workshops.

He told our reporter that to move everything from his present premises is a venture that will tell heavily on his purse.

"I have some thousands of pounds worth of material to be moved from this shop and this cannot be done overnight," he said.

Mr. Seabela's success in life dates back to the first days of hi arrival in Johannesburg, 30 years ago.

Young Mr. Seabela arrived in the Golden City, to seek a job.

where he worked for a number of years.

Through his hard work he was made head boss-boy of the firm.

But the idead of having a printing press came to Mr. Seabela while he worked for the "Daily Express".

In 1946 he took over from its proprietors, the Victory Press.

There are 17 Africans employed by Mr. Seabela in his modern shop.

In the heart of the city, he gets his electric current easily

**Fired shot at party**
— Witness

Two clerks, employed by Mr. Seabela, at work at his press. They are Mrs. M. P. ..dla and Mrs. N. Boyang. Right: A worker busy on one of the big printing machines at the Victory Press. Below right: Mr. Seabela.

---

The *Rand Daily Mail* reported in April 1957 that the duo had managed Victory Press for 16 years on Main Street in central Johannesburg. However, due to the racist law, they were convicted for illegally occupying space in violation of the Group Areas Act. The fines were suspended for three years, provided they vacated the premises by June 1958.[5]

The court had been informed that Victory Press's printing machinery was valued at about £5 000.[6] The enforced move out of the Johannesburg central business district was very inconvenient, not to mention the harassment by apartheid authorities and the cost of moving heavy machinery.

Seabela also faced the challenge of providing electricity at his new location in Orlando, as the townships were not electrified.[7]

The removal of black traders from areas designated for *"whites only"* often hindered black-owned businesses from conveniently reaching their customers.

Seabela passed away on July 25, 1975, at 70 years of age. He left behind his wife, Ntebatse Ruth Seabela, and his adult children, Moses, Virginia, and Peter. At the time of his death, he was residing in Mofolo Central, Soweto, and was known as a business owner.[8]

5  Rand Daily Mail, Two Non-European Business Men Fined, 18 April 1957, p4
6  Rand Daily Mail, Two Non-European Business Men Fined, 18 April 1957, p4
7  Wits Historical Papers Research Archive, Bantu World newspaper, 1935-1955, From kitchen boy to head of firm---- now he has to move, 24 December 1955, p2
8  National Archives of South Africa, NI/4/3-1601/75, Death Notice, Estate File Maphoko Petrus Seabela

Upon PK Seabela's death, his eldest son, Moses, instructed the law firm Edward Nathan Friedland, Mansell & Lewis to settle the estate.[9] The law firm later evolved into Edward Nathan Sonnenbergs (ENS). According to PK Seabela's estate file, he held a life policy with Home Trust Lewens, valued at R3 168.19.

A note from Barclays National Bank to the Commissioner of Bantu Administration and Developments, dated August 25, 1975, indicated that Seabela was the sole proprietor of Victory Press and held a current account with Barclays. A certificate of balance, dated the same day, showed Victory Press had R953.26 in the bank.[10]

# CONCLUSION

The story of Seabela illuminates the broader struggle of black entrepreneurs during the apartheid era in South Africa. Despite his relentless ambition and success in establishing Victory Press, the Group Areas Act served as a constant barrier, embodying the systemic racism that permeated every aspect of life during that time. Seabela's forced relocation from Johannesburg's central business district was more than an inconvenient move; it was a manifestation of the societal oppression that hindered the growth and development of black-owned businesses. His life, marked by both triumph and struggle, stands as a testament to the resilience and creativity of those who fought against racial discrimination.

The legacy of Seabela continues to resonate, providing a stark reminder of the challenges faced, and the courage displayed, by black entrepreneurs in a deeply divided society.

9   National Archives of South Africa, N1/4/3-1601/75, Letter by Edward Nathan Friedland Mansell & Lewis to Bantu Affairs Commission, Estates Department, Estate File Maphoko Petrus Seabela
10  National Archives of South Africa, N1/4/3-1601/75, Estate File Maphoko Petrus Seabela

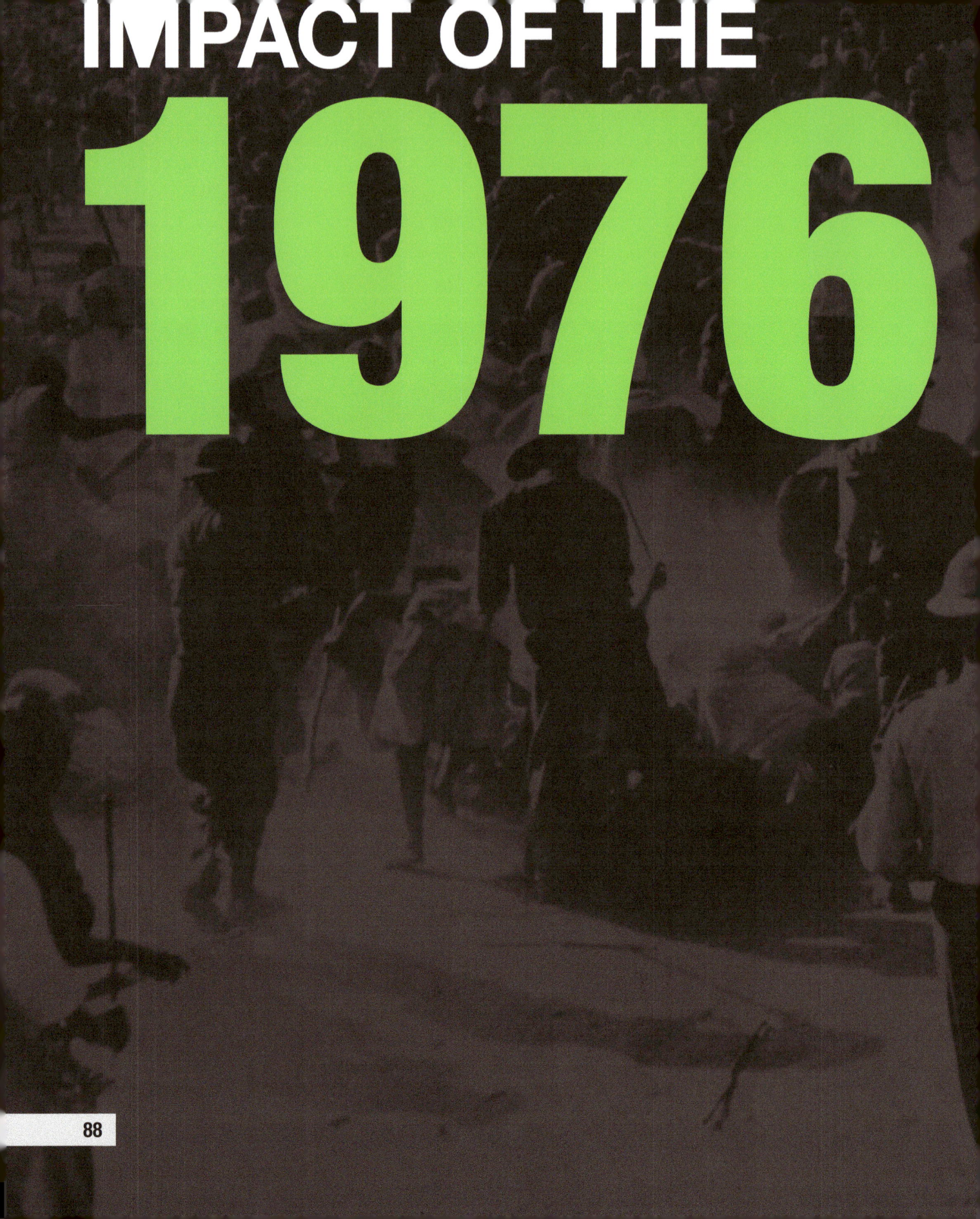

# IMPACT OF THE
# 1976

# RIOTS

## ON BLACK BUSINESSES:
### THE STORY OF LAWRENCE MALINDI

The multi-million-rand losses incurred by black business people during the tragic riots of June 16, 1976, stand as a relatively untold chapter in South African history. Black business people found themselves as collateral damage when thousands of black youths took to the streets that day to protest against the racist apartheid regime. These young people were rallying against substandard education and the imposition of Afrikaans as a mandatory language of instruction for African people.

Lawrence Malindi, a general dealer in Soweto, became one of the many black entrepreneurs who suffered financial losses due to the resistance against the unjust apartheid government. Malindi operated a retail business, trading under Ntsele General Dealer at 2400 Orlando East, Soweto, Johannesburg.

On March 22, 1976, Malindi had entered into an agreement with Afribank Insurance Brokers for a fire insurance policy valued at R50 000, covering the loss or destruction to the property of the business. Malindi's understanding of the agreement was that his business would be protected against loss, destruction, or damage caused by fire to the property, regardless of its origin. This included any loss, destruction of or damage to the shop resulting from or instigated by rioting or riotous behaviour. The insurance policy was effective upon payment of the annual premium of R383.80c on March 22, 1976.

Afribank Insurance Brokers subsequently secured a fire policy from Shield Insurance Company, with coverage extending from May 8, 1976 to May 8, 1977.

However, Malindi later discovered, much to his dismay and in what he argued was a breach of his agreement with Afribank Insurance Brokers; that the policy offered by Shield Insurance Company contained an exclusion clause. This exclusion denied coverage for damage, destruction, or loss arising from warlike operations, mutiny, riot, military or popular uprising, insurrection, rebellion, revolution, usurped power, or state of siege.

## ON JUNE 17, MALINDI'S NTSELE GENERAL DEALER WAS DESTROYED BY FIRE CAUSED BY THE RIOTS, LEADING HIM TO SUBMIT A CLAIM OF R50 000. SHIELD INSURANCE COMPANY, HOWEVER, REJECTED THE CLAIM, STATING THAT THE DAMAGE WAS RIOT-RELATED AND THUS EXCLUDED FROM COVERAGE UNDER THE POLICY.[1]

Malindi's business misfortune was merely a small part of the wider economic destruction that resulted from the resistance to apartheid racism. A month after the June 16, 1976 riots, a provisional tally showed 51 damaged shops, most of which were completely destroyed, with millions of rands in inventory and expensive equipment lost. The devastation affected various businesses, including grocers, general dealers, dry cleaners, eating houses, and fish and chips shops.[2]

[1] National Archives of South Africa Wit Dept 730/77. Illiquid Case Payment Lawrence Malindi versus Afribank Insurance Brokers (PHC) PRTL MY71 LTD. In the Matter Between Lawrence Malindi (Plaintiff) and Afribank Insurance Brokers (Defendant). Particulars of Plaintiff's Claim. p1-9.
[2] Own Correspondent, Rand Daily Mail. "Riot damage is a shock for Soweto", Thursday, July 22, 1976. p12. line1 p2.

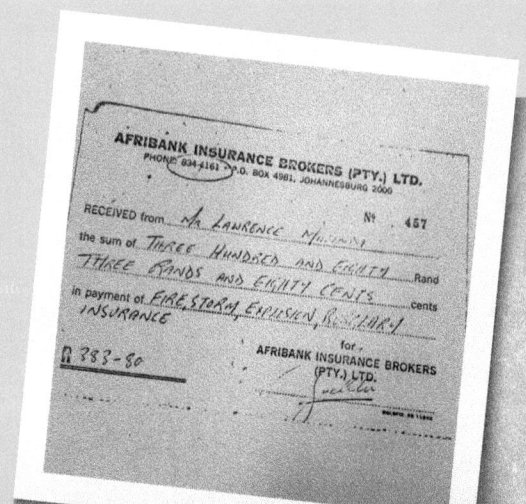

*"For many shopkeepers, their businesses were their only livelihood, which they had built up over many years. Some were insured, but insurance companies are refusing to pay for riot damages,"* TJ Makhaya, the then Mayor of Soweto and chairman of the Urban Bantu Council, as cited in the *Rand Daily Mail.*[3]

# PROTRACTED LEGAL BATTLE OVER INSURANCE DISPUTE

When Malindi sought an insurance claim for the loss of his business assets, he was met with a demanding request from the lawyers of Afribank Insurance Brokers. He was asked to prepare a substantial bundle of paperwork. The exhaustive list of details and documents required by Webber Wentzel & Co, the legal representatives of the Afribank Insurance Brokers, encompassed various aspects. These included the ownership details of the shop building, the goods inside, fixtures and fittings on the premises, details of the insurance agreement, the issuer of the fire insurance, a thorough account of the loss and destruction, the cause of the fire, and clarification on what was meant by riot and riotous behaviour.[4]

In providing the particulars, Malindi demonstrated that he had started his business in 1964. As of June 16, 1976, the trading account for the business showed stocks on hand valued at R13 375, buildings worth R25 200, furniture and equipment amounting to R7 538.75c, and machinery valued at R3 325c.

He indicated that the fire had started at approximately 09:00am on June 17, 1976. There were riots in the vicinity of the shop building where the fire broke out. During the pandemonium, Soweto's citizens injured individuals and sometimes attacked and burnt down buildings and shops. The stock, fixtures, fittings, and the buildings themselves were all consumed by the flames.[5]

4   National Archives of South Africa, W.L.D. 6750/77, Illiquid Case Payment Lawrence Malindi versus Afribank Insurance Brokers (PROPRIETARY) LTD. In the Matter Between Lawrence Malindi (Plaintiff) and Afribank Insurance Brokers (Defendant), Request for Further Particulars, July 12, 1977
5   Ibid, Plaintiffs reply to the Defendants request for further particulars for purposes of trial, March 29, 1979

The goods lost to the fire at Ntsele General Dealers included food stocks, fruit and vegetables, fresh and prepared meat, mineral water, daily products, toiletries, patent medicine and cosmetics. The inferno also consumed various pieces of furniture and equipment, such as desks, chairs, tables, food and fridge counters, fish and chips fryer, glass display cabinets, wall shelves, electrical fittings and sanitaryware. Malindi promptly reported the destruction to the Afribank Insurance Brokers, expecting that as brokers, they would file a claim with Shield Insurance Company. When Afribank Insurance Brokers initiated the claim, they were informed by Shield Insurance Company that it had been rejected.

Malindi subsequently provided financial statements of accounts for the business. As of June 16, 1976, the financial books indicated that Ntsele General Dealers & Butchery had a gross profit of R5 705.75c and a net profit of R3 200. The bulk of the costs were wages of R1 300, followed by rent at R240, water and lights at R120; the balance comprised various expenses, such as painting of the premises, sharpening of knives, telephone fees, advertising, bookkeeping charges and so on.[6]

However, Webber Wentzel & Co still required more documentation from Malindi. This additional paperwork included the ledger, journals, cashbook, invoices, bank account, tax returns and assessment for the tax years ended February 28 in 1975, 1976 and 1977. Lease agreements were also requested.[7] Some of the documents were provided, but others were still outstanding and were reported to have been destroyed by the fire.[8]

Over the years, Malindi had struggled to provide some of the documents, leading to multiple instances where the court was requested to grant an order compelling him to issue the paperwork and to pay the costs of the court application.[9] The court later granted an order for Malindi to issue the papers without delay and pay the costs of the application.[10]

The legal costs imposed on Malindi, due to the delayed provision of documents, had by then risen to R260.28c, and he had only paid R10. Consequently, the sheriff was asked to attach his assets.[11]

In August 1979, the sheriff went to the address where Malindi's Ntsele General Dealers had traded in Orlando to enforce an attachment of assets. However, he was unable to find Malindi or attach anything, as the only thing visible to the sheriff's eyes was a burnt-down store.[12] The sheriff was then directed to search for Malindi and attach assets at another address. It seemed Malindi had moved and was now operating another enterprise called P. Phinda General Dealer & Eating House Shop 4, 54a, Zone 4 in Meadowlands, Johannesburg.[13] The sheriff proceeded to attach assets in the Meadowlands shop, including a till counter, a warmer, medicine and cake cabinets, tins of polish, coffee, sweets, fruit; 240 packets of washing powder, 48 packets of sugar and 120 cakes of toilet soaps.[14]

## THE MATTER HAD DRAGGED ON FOR OVER THREE YEARS IN COURT. FINALLY, ON OCTOBER 30, 1979, MALINDI'S LEGAL REPRESENTATIVES WROTE TO THE REGISTRAR OF THE SUPREME COURT OF SOUTH AFRICA, ADVISING THE COURT THAT THEY WERE WITHDRAWING THE CASE AS THE MATTER HAD BEEN SETTLED BETWEEN THE TWO PARTIES.[15]

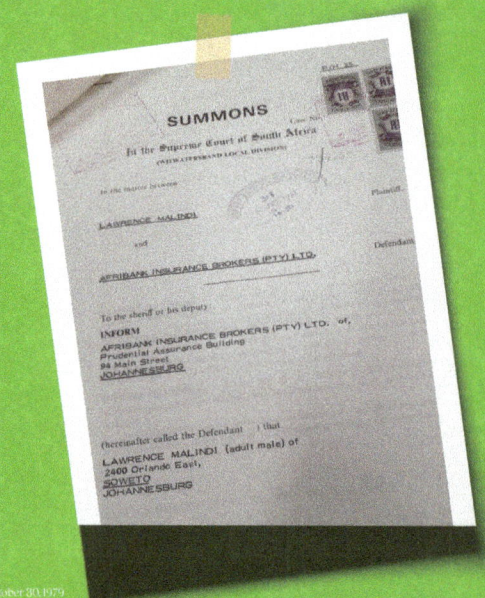

Ibid. Further Particulars, October 26, 1977
Ibid. Notice in Terms of Rule 35 (13) of the Rules of the Court, January 9, 1979
Ibid. Plaintiff's Reply to the Defendant's Request For Further Particulars For Purposes of Trial, March 29, 1979
Ibid. September 27, 1977
Ibid. Court Order, April 3, 1979

Ibid. Writ of Execution, July 23, 1979
Ibid. Writ of Execution, August 2, 1979
Ibid. Writ of Execution, August 15, 1979
Ibid. Writ of Execution, August 22, 1979
Ibid. Notice of Withdrawal of Action, October 30, 1979

# CONCLUSION

This story of Malindi's business misfortune paints a vivid picture of the broader tragedy that many black business owners faced in the wake of the June 16, 1976 riots. His experience illustrates the broader struggles faced by many black business owners during the turbulent period of resistance against apartheid in South Africa. The tale of lost livelihoods, protracted legal battles, and insurance disputes, casts a sombre reflection on a turbulent time in South Africa's history. After years of protracted legal proceedings and personal hardship, including the seizure of assets from his new venture, Malindi finally reached a settlement with the insurance company. His story serves as a poignant reminder of the complex and often devastating interplay between political upheaval, systemic barriers, and individual entrepreneurship.

# SAM MOTSUENYANE

## THE QUINTESSENTIAL FOUNDER OF ENTERPRISES AND LEADER

Under difficult circumstances, Samuel Mokgethi *"Sam"* Motsuenyane successfully spearheaded the formation of multiple businesses and black economic advancement organisations from scratch. A pioneer in black economic advancement, he courageously led black business people into previously unchartered commercial territories, traditionally considered the exclusive domain of white people in South Africa.

The drive that propelled him to lead in the establishment of several enterprises could arguably be attributed to his roots in a farming community, personal struggles in securing employment during his youth, endurance through racially challenging work conditions, and exposure to black entrepreneurs who had embarked on their business journeys ahead of him.

In the face of rigid apartheid policies in South Africa during his early years, Motsuenyane founded a diverse range of enterprises, including a cartage business, a nursery concern selling flowers, trees and landscaping services; a banking institution that continues to thrive almost 30 years since its establishment. Under Motsuenyane's leadership, NAFCOC initiated ventures in insurance, construction and a substantial supermarket chain. In the 1970s, Motsuenyane became the founding chairman of a medical scheme designed to cater to the underserviced medical needs of black people.

# A CHALLENGING BEGINNING
## BIRTH AND EARLY LIFE

Motsuenyane's journey began under harsh circumstances. He was born on a farm called Eignaarsfontein, in the Potchefstroom area, where his parents toiled as sharecroppers. Being a sharecropper meant labouring on the land and giving a third of the harvest to the farm owner, as part of rent, while retaining the rest for consumption and potential commercial use.

AN Gadi family archives

Legend has it that Motsuenyane's birth was a difficult one. In the absence of medical professionals to assist with the delivery, a priest was called upon to invoke divine intervention. Elderly women in the community were also called in for assistance. Fortunately, Motsuenyane made it into the world healthy and strong. The priest suggested that the arduous birth indicated the arrival of a person destined for greatness. However, Motsuenyane's mother withheld this story from him, fearing it might inflate his ego and encourage arrogance.[1]

Born on February 11, 1927, in Potchefstroom in the Transvaal, Motsuenyane went on to do his primary schooling at Wallmansthal in Pretoria between 1938 and 1943. He then proceeded to attend the Wilberforce Institute for his secondary education from 1944 to 1946, demonstrating diligence and commitment to his studies. Motsuenyane worked hard to attain his senior certificate by correspondence from 1947-1948.[2]

As he had to work while attending school, Motsuenyane completed his schooling as a part-time learner. At the age of 20, his father gave him an old bicycle for him to travel to Johannesburg in search of employment – a more cost-efficient means than paying bus fare. Three months later, he found a job as an *"office boy"* and messenger at a yarn factory called President Knitting Mills, situated on the then President Street in Johannesburg. His responsibilities included making tea for the directors and factory staff, collecting the mail from the Post Office and preparing soap parcels for the employees. Unfortunately, his tenure at the mill was short-lived following allegations of theft by a colleague.

After losing his job at the mill, Motsuenyane faced a difficult few months trying to find another job. Eventually, he found one at a toy manufacturing company, where he had to scrape rust metal used to make toys. Unlike his co-workers who spent their lunch breaks playing games, Motsuenyane used this time to focus on his schoolbooks from the Lyceum Correspondence College. However, misfortune struck again when he was retrenched from the toy manufacturer, forcing him to cycle around Johannesburg once more, in search of employment.[3]

Motsuenyane, S. A Testament of Hope: The Autobiography of Dr Sam Motsuenyane, p68.
L MSA Archives. ACC2501 "Who's the President", Report by FK Dumede, Vice-President NAFCOC, June 17, 1974, p3.
Motsuenyane, S. A Testament of Hope: The Autobiography of Dr Sam Motsuenyane, p68.

National Archives of South Africa: Sam Motsuenyane in his office: SAB, 18343

Cycling around Johannesburg, Motsuenyane found his movements restricted. He was accused of violating pass laws and subsequently arrested. After being held in a police station for about 14 days while awaiting trial, he eventually appeared in court and was released. To avoid another violation of pass laws, he needed to secure employment within two weeks after his release. Motsuenyane was eventually hired as a cleaner and tea-maker at a shop in Orange Grove, Johannesburg, but his tenure there was also short-lived: this time due to the ill-treatment he encountered. After another extended period of job hunting and paging through newspaper advertisements, he landed a job at African Sewing Machines, a repairer and seller of sewing machines.

Here, he worked as an *"office boy"*-cum-messenger. However, a troubling incident where he was falsely accused of theft, assaulted by one of the directors, and subsequently imprisoned, led him to leave the job.

He was imprisoned just as he was preparing for his senior certificate examination. He attributed this unfortunate event to the malice of some individuals. After this ordeal, he made a personal vow never to work for a white man again. By the end of 1948, he had taken his senior certificate examination and passed.[4] Motsuenyane then pursued a Diploma in Social Work from the Jan H. Hofmeyer School of Social Work, which he successfully completed in 1951.[5]

During his time at Jan H. Hofmeyr, he encountered several business people in Johannesburg through the Moral Re-Armament (MRA), religious platform. These included Cyril Pearce, the chairman of the Johannesburg Chamber of Commerce, and Soweto entrepreneur Paul Mosaka. Mosaka was reputedly staunchly opposed to the MRA's efforts, as he believed it made African leaders submissive amidst the brutal apartheid regime. Motsuenyane also had his own reservations, but seemed to respect the business leaders involved with the MRA activities, including JCP Mavimbela, SJJ Lesolang, Ben Mabuza, JM Mohlala and Bigvai Masekela.[6]

Motsuenyane, SM. A Testament of Hope: The Autobiography of Dr Sam Motsuenyane, p122.
UNISA Archives, AGG292, "Who is the Treasurer?" Report by UG Ginwede, Vice President NAFCOC, June 17, 1974, p4.
Motsuenyane, S. A Testament of Hope: The Autobiography of Dr Sam Motsuenyane, p61.

# Starting the African National Soil Conservation Association (ANSCA)

Following his education, Motsuenyane embarked on his career as the National Organising Secretary of the African National Soil Conservation Association (ANSCA), an institution he helped establish.[7]

His involvement in ANSCA's formation stemmed from his work at the National Veld Trust, which aimed to launch soil conservation projects in black communities. Motsuenyane was deployed to the Transkei to engage black leaders on their thoughts about establishing an independent soil conservation project. Some of these discussions proved challenging as he heard first-hand how black people had been forced by government to cull their animals to rehabilitate the land. Some people believed that erosion could be mitigated if black people were given more land. After extensive dialogue with farmers and community leaders in the Transkei, Motsuenyane compiled a report

endorsing the establishment of an organisation to address soil erosion. In response, the National Veld Trust committed £40 000 to this initiative, which would be named ANSCA.

WB Ngakane, a former educator and politician from Soweto, was elected as President; JM Mohlala, a businessman from KwaThema in Springs, as Deputy President, and Motsuenyane himself as the National Organising Secretary. One of his responsibilities was to promote ANSCA within black communities and dispel misconceptions that the organisation was an agent of the Native Affairs Department. Over time, ANSCA evolved to focus on educating the youth about soil conservation.[8]

It was during his early professional working life that Motsuenyane met his wife, Jocelyn Nomgqibelo Mashinini. The couple got married in 1954.[9]

[7] UNISA Archives AC02261 "Who is the Treasurer" Report by FG Guniode, Vice President, NAFCOC June 17, 1954. p3
[8] Motsuenyane, S. A Testament of Hope. The Autobiography of Dr Sam Motsuenyane. p42-50
[9] Motsuenyane, S. A Testament of Hope. The Autobiography of Dr Sam Motsuenyane. p54-65

# ESTABLISHING BAMPA SYNDICATE
# A VENTURE INTO THE CARTAGE BUSINESS

In 1955, shortly after his marriage, Motsuenyane co-founded Bampa Syndicate, a cartage company, alongside businessman and NAFCOC leader Bigvai Masekela, who served as the chairman while Motsuenyane assumed the role of secretary. The construction boom in Soweto at the time opened up opportunities for truck owners to transport bricks, cement and other building materials. During this period, the Johannesburg City Council was persuaded to use black-owned lorries. Bampa Syndicate procured trucks on a hire purchase agreement for this purpose. However, work soon dried up. Motsuenyane attributed some of these challenges to corrupt officials who favoured truck owners willing to pay bribes. Consequently, amid financial difficulties, four of the six trucks that the Bampa Syndicate had acquired, were repossessed. This period coincided with Motsuenyane's preparations to leave for the US.[10]

As he prepared to travel across the Atlantic, ANSCA also faced struggles. Despite conducting workshops on land use and emphasising the connection between agriculture and economic development, the organisation encountered funding challenges. Motsuenyane would later recall that after fundraising efforts in black communities and appeals for financial aid from the Department of Native Agriculture, the government wanted ANSCA to operate along ethnic lines in the homelands.

Motsuenyane rejected this and a decision was taken to dissolve ANSCA, which closed in 1959 just as he was about to leave for the US.[11]

In the US, Motsuenyane studied for a Bachelor of Science in Agriculture at the University of North Carolina, completing his degree in 1962. Upon his return from the US after his studies, he became involved in agricultural development activities. In 1964, he was a founding member of NAFCOC. He also assumed editorship of *NAFCOC News* and *The African Trader.*[12]

Motsuenyane, S. A Testament of Hope: The Autobiography of Dr Sam Motsuenyane, p52.
Motsuenyane, S. A Testament of Hope: The Autobiography of Dr Sam Motsuenyane, p52-53.
ANSA Archives. AG2510 "Who is the Treasurer", Report by PG Gumede, Vice President NAFCOC, 17 June 1959, p1.

# OPENING A NURSERY AND LANDSCAPING BUSINESS IN SOWETO

After returning from the US soon after completing his studies, Motsuenyane was offered a job as an agricultural officer by the Department of Bantu Agriculture. Despite financial constraints, he declined the offer, knowing that taking up employment with a department unpopular with black people would be challenging. Instead, he used his knowledge in horticulture to start a small nursery in Soweto.

However, as black people faced restrictions in urban areas, including limited access to land and restrictions on the type of businesses they could legally establish, Motsuenyane had to devise an alternative plan. He approached a Mr Levine, who owned land in Moroka, Soweto, and asked for permission to rent a plot to start the nursery. To deflect any questions from the authorities, the understanding would be that Motsuenyane was merely working for Mr Levine, and did not own the business.[1]

Motsuenyane started selling trees and flowers to people of Rockville and other townships, and also offered landscaping services. His clientele included schools, churches and homeowners. Eventually, he could afford to purchase a Bedford truck in addition to the Kombi he had already acquired for transporting plants. As people built new homes, they sought Motsuenyane's landscaping expertise.

When the nursery was started, Bampa Syndicate, co-founded with Masekela, was generating modest income, aiding Motsuenyane in starting the nursery. Upon his return from the US, Motsuenyane found Masekela serving as secretary of the Johannesburg African Chamber of Commerce (JACOC) with Richard Maponya as chairman. Both Maponya and Masekela were instrumental in expanding JACOC beyond Soweto, and leading the formation of NAFCOC in 1964 where Maponya was elected president. With his international experience and ownership of a nursery business, Motsuenyane was invited to address NAFCOC about agriculture. This was the beginning of his long relationship with the organisation.[2]

Motsuenyane, S, A Testament of Hope: The Autobiography of Dr Sam Motsuenyane, 130-140
Motsuenyane, S, A Testament of Hope: The Autobiography of Dr Sam Motsuenyane, 140

# FORCED RELOCATION FROM SOWETO TO RURAL BOPHUTHATSWANA

In the course of cultivating his nursery business, Motsuenyane soon attracted the attention of the apartheid authorities and their security establishment. After being monitored by the security establishment, he was summoned to the Department of Bantu Agriculture in Pretoria. There he was questioned about his decision to operate a nursery in Soweto; an activity, which as a black person, he was not permitted to do. Motsuenyane was told if he wanted to continue operating his nursery business without being arrested, he would need to relocate to the Bophuthatswana homeland.

So, in 1965, he left Johannesburg and settled on the Klipgat farm near Winterveld in rural Bophuthatswana. The Department of Native Agriculture granted him a 10-year lease on the farm. Motsuenyane had to build a new home for his family, as the farmhouse on the property was in disrepair, having been abandoned by the white farmer who had previously owned it. The upside was that the land was bigger; approximately 30 hectares. Seizing the opportunity, Motsuenyane expanded his farming operations, planting vegetables and starting a poultry business. The vegetables were supplied to the Pretoria Fresh Produce Market. He became involved in efforts to organise local farmers to showcase their produce.[15]

In 1967, he founded the Winterveld Farmers' Association and was elected President of NAFCOC the following year. Motsuenyane served on numerous boards, including as director of the South African Intermediate Technology Group and as a member of the board of trustees of the South African Foundation.[16]

At NAFCOC, one of Motsuenyane's tasks was to produce a monthly newsletter called the *African Trader,* established in 1967. Despite his efforts to write articles and source advertising, he struggled to attract funding and interest from many white businesses. Consequently, the publication had to be discontinued due to lack of funding.[17]

15 Motsuenyane, S. A Testament of Hope: The Autobiography of Dr Sam Motsuenyane, p118
16 UNISA Archives, ACC830, "Who's the Provider?" Report by T.G Gumede, Vice President NAFCOC, 17 June 1974, p5
17 Motsuenyane, S. A Testament of Hope: The Autobiography of Dr Sam Motsuenyane, p63

# PIONEERING THE ESTABLISHMENT OF AFRICAN BANK

In 1972, Motsuenyane, along with other NAFCOC members toured Europe. During this trip, he requested a meeting with the leadership of Barclays in London. In a discussion with Barclays about the establishment of African Bank, the London-based bank agreed to support the vision. Barclays committed to training staff for African Bank and assisting with the necessary capital to launch it, pending government approval. Motsuenyane also initiated discussions with the then South African Finance Minister, Dr Nico Diederichs, to secure government approval for the registration of African Bank. The necessary approvals were granted.[18]

Before the launch of African Bank, Motsuenyane visited the US to seek insights from black business leaders there. He visited North Carolina Mutual, which was then the largest black insurance company in the US, and paid a visit to Farmers and Mechanics Bank. He also met with National Bankers Association, an association of black financial institutions, and invited its president, Dr Edward Irons, to address the 11th NAFCOC conference in Phuthaditjhaba in 1975 and share the experience of black Americans in the banking sector.

To gain practical training in the operational principles of running a bank, Motsuenyane also served on the board of directors of the Hill Samuel Bank, a British merchant bank operating in South Africa, from 1974 to 1978. This experience proved invaluable when he assumed the role of chairman of African Bank in 1975.[19]

In 1979, to further enhance his understanding of banking, Motsuenyane was offered a training opportunity by Chase Manhattan Bank in New York, where he spent three months studying its operations. He regarded this exercise as another valuable opportunity to make him a better-informed chairman of African Bank.[20]

# HEADING SIZWE MEDICAL FUND

The Sizwe Medical Fund was established by a group of medical doctors, including the then-detained activist Dr Nthato Motlana, Dr Abner Tlakula of Tembisa, Dr Ndumiso Mzamane of Katlehong, and Dr Phaki Mokhesi of Sharpeville. Motsuenyane was selected to lead the endeavour as chairman.[21]

18 Motsuenyane, S. A Testament of Hope: The Autobiography of Dr Sam Motsuenyane, p100-101.
19 Motsuenyane, S. A Testament of Hope: The Autobiography of Dr Sam Motsuenyane, p109.
20 Motsuenyane, S. A Testament of Hope: The Autobiography of Dr Sam Motsuenyane, p78.
21 Staff Reporter, Rand Daily Mail, Medical aid for blacks, Tuesday, March 21, 1978, p6.

# NAVIGATING THE COMPLEXITIES OF INTERNATIONAL PARTNERSHIPS: MOTSUENYANE'S EXPERIENCE WITH LIFE INSURANCE

On February 4, 1979, *The Sunday Times* reported a noteworthy business collaboration involving Motsuenyane, US company Sentry Life and Permanent Life Assurance, with NAFCOC also a key player. Motsuenyane was invited to join the Permanent Life Assurance board, which had a significant history with NAFCOC.[22] NAFCOC had owned shares in a joint venture with Permanent Life. However, the Permanent Life business was acquired by Sentry Life.[23]

Previously, NAFCOC had owned shares in a joint venture with Permanent Life, which had culminated in the formation of NAFCOC Permanent Life Assurance Company. The goal was to expand the company's reach by selling insurance policies to the black population. However, the majority of Permanent Life's shareholders sold their stakes to Sentry Life Assurance, leading to a takeover.

After the takeover, there was an agreement that Sentry Life Assurance would use its technical expertise to manage the newly-formed NAFCOC Sentry Company. As Sentry Life Assurance was based in the US, Motsuenyane, as director in the partnership, would fly to the US for board meetings. He would recount that when he landed in the US, he would fly as a solo passenger on a private plane sent by the Sentry Life Assurance leader.

However, political pressures soon strained the partnership. Calls for sanctions against apartheid South Africa mounted, pressurising international companies, including Sentry, to disinvest from South Africa. At a meeting in the US, a decision to disinvest was taken. Motsuenyane made futile attempts to source funding for NAFCOC to buy the shares it did not own in the partnership. To his dismay, Sentry sold the joint company to African Life Insurance. Motsuenyane recalled that the entire company was taken over against their will and NAFCOC could not do much without funds.[24]

Wilkinson in *Sunday Times*, 'US Firm to Sell Insurance in SA', January 4 1979, p.
*Rand Daily Mail*, 'NAFCOC gets different point', Thursday, June 28, 1979, p.
Motsuenyane, S. A Testament of Hope: The Autobiography of Dr Sam Motsuenyane, p141.

# PIONEERING A CONSTRUCTION JOINT VENTURE

In 1977, Motsuenyane was elected chairman of the newly formed African Development Construction Company. The company was conceived as a joint venture between NAFCOC and Roberts Construction Company. Leo Schreider from Roberts Construction Company was appointed as the general manager. The ownership structure was such that NAFCOC held a majority stake of 51%, while Roberts Construction Company controlled the remaining 49%.[25]

# ADVOCATING FOR RACIAL EQUALITY IN THE RETAIL SECTOR

During Motsuenyane's presidency, NAFCOC collaborated with numerous white-controlled businesses. However, a proposed partnership with the supermarket chain Pick n Pay, failed to gain sufficient support. The head of Pick n Pay, Raymond Ackerman, had proposed a deal that would allow black business people to own a controlling share of the venture in black residential areas, while NAFCOC would hold a minority share in Pick n Pay operations in white areas.[26]

Motsuenyane, however, stated that there were concerns that this partnership would be limited to black townships alone. NAFCOC members believed that such a partnership should extend to the central business district in Johannesburg as well.[27]

*"There should, in fact, be far greater agitation today for the opening of central business district areas to black businessmen, as blacks are responsible for almost 50% of the total income accruing to those areas. This is quite logical because the black working population spends most of its time in the white areas,"* Motsuenyane was quoted as saying in the *Rand Daily Mail.*[28]

Later, NAFCOC took steps to establish its own mega supermarket and retail commercial property venture, known as the Black Chain. However, Motsuenyane did not head this initiative – the leadership role was taken up by fellow NAFCOC leader Solomon Joel Jack Lesolang.[29]

25 Skhosana, n. *Rand Daily Mail*, NAFCOC Company Awarded Contract, Monday January 16, 1978. p1.
26 DOUGH, *This Paper Thing*, Pick 'N Pay Shelves Black chain plan, July 12, 1979. p1.
27 Motsuenyane, s.A. *Testament of Hope: The autobiography of Dr. Sam Motsuenyane*, p7.
28 *Rand Daily Mail*, Let the Kaffers into city centres, July 7, 1979.
29 Staff Reporter, r. Black Chain gives top project, *Rand Daily Mail*, June 27, 1979. p4.

# ACTIVISM AGAINST APARTHEID:
# A STAND FOR JUSTICE AND EQUALITY

In 1976, when many Bantustans were embroiled in discussions over the *"independence"* granted to homelands, Motsuenyane publicly voiced his opposition. Lucas Mangope, the Chief Minister of Bophuthatswana, reportedly retaliated to these comments, threatening to retract privileges extended to NAFCOC and to counter any opposition to independence. The *Rand Daily Mail* would report that Mangope had threatened to replace African Bank with a *"Tswana-controlled bank"*.[30]

In 1977, Motsuenyane stepped down from the council of the South Africa Foundation, a lobby group which called for cooperation between black and white business to secure the big economic interests, and was led by businessman Basel Hersov. His departure was due to the foundation's failure to condemn the government's banning of black organisations and detention of leaders. Motsuenyane felt he could no longer associate with the foundation, as it did not seem capable of fostering change, and his credibility in the black community could have been compromised.[31]

October 19, 1977, known as Black Wednesday in South Africa, marked the government's ban of *The World and Weekend World newspapers* for reporting on the atrocious activities by the apartheid regime. The editor of *The World*, Percy Qoboza, was detained for five months. Following Steve Biko's murder in September 1977, nearly 20 Black Consciousness organisations were declared illegal and scores of political activists detained.[32]

At a function celebrating the 5th anniversary of African Bank, Motsuenyane publicly criticised Mangope for preventing African Bank from registering bonds in excess of R500 000. Motsuenyane argued that white financial institutions were given preferential treatment and allowed to register bonds, while African Bank and many black companies faced restrictions. In his address, Motsuenyane informed the audience that the government had been petitioned to revoke restrictions hindering the economic development of black companies, but that all attempts had been unsuccessful. One of the legislations restricting African Bank and black people in the homeland was the Bophuthatswana Land Control Act,[33] which included restrictions such as no person being allowed to acquire more than one residential site and either one business or other site without ministerial approval.[34]

In 1986, Motsuenyane's house was bombed, and his wife arrested due to their perceived association with a group of youth in Winterveld opposing apartheid. Between 1986 and 1987, the Motsuenyanes lived in a caravan as they worked to rebuild their home.[35]

[30] Motsuenyane, J. Rand Daily Mail, NAFCOC president to reply to chief Mangope's threat, December 8, 1976, p24.
[31] Sasha, E. Rand Daily Mail, Motsuenyane quits over the Bantustan, Friday March 17, 1978, p2.
[32] South African History Online, Black Wednesday: The banning of 19 Black Conscious Movement Organisations.
https://www.sahistory.org.za/dated-event/black-wednesday-banning-19-black-conscious-movement-organisations
[33] Mangope, L. Rand Daily Mail, Mangope imposes bond unfair restrictions, Monday, January 10, 1981, p4.
[34] Section 18 of the Bophuthatswana Land Control Act No.39 of 1979, Restrictions upon acquisition of land, p25.
[35] Motsuenyane, S. A Testament of Hope, The Autobiography of Dr Sam Motsuenyane, 2016, p121-128.

# A TRUSTED LEADER IN ESTABLISHED WHITE-CONTROLLED COMPANIES

Motsuenyane was considered a reliable leader in numerous corporate boards from 1986 to 1996, including many traditionally white-controlled businesses. One such business was Barlow Rand, now known as Barloworld, where Motsuenyane served as a director. Under his guidance, NAFCOC and Barlow Rand collaborated to aid emerging small black industrialists.

From 1980 to 1991, Motsuenyane was also a director at the Small Business Development Corporation, now known as Business Partners. He held directorships at First National Bank from 1986 to 1992, and served on the board of Transnet between 1989 and 1994. Motsuenyane was also part of the Independent Development Trust between 1989 and 1996, chaired the Venda Development Corporation from 1992-1994 and served Allianz Insurance from 1993-1994.

In addition to his local arrangements, Motsuenyane also worked with the Paris-based International Chamber of Commerce, extending his influence globally. With the advent of democracy in 1994, he resigned from many of the boards he had served on, to assume his role as a member of parliament. In 1996, he stepped down from all the remaining boards, upon his appointment by Nelson Mandela as Ambassador to Saudi Arabia.[36]

Motsuenyane's bold journey through the business world left an indelible mark. Indeed, the prophecy at his difficult birth — that he would become a significant figure — undoubtedly manifested. His profound influence in business and his vast global networks were truly beyond imagination.

**He died on 29 April 2024 at the age of 97.**

## CONCLUSION

Sam Motsuenyane's life-story stands as a profound testament to resilience, vision, and unswerving commitment to social empowerment. Rising from humble beginnings and confronting the harsh realities of apartheid-era South Africa, he managed to co-found and lead businesses that transcended mere profit-making, to embody instead a broader mission of community upliftment. His contributions to banking, entrepreneurship and activism not only broke racial barriers, but laid foundations that continue to thrive decades later. Driven by a firm belief in merit, equality, and self-reliance, Motsuenyane's legacy persists as an inspiring beacon for generations of African leaders and entrepreneurs to come. His life's journey, marked by both adversity and triumph, encapsulates the quintessential spirit of determination and innovation.

36. Motsuenyane, S. A Testament of Hope: The Autobiography of Dr Sam Motsuenyane p111-113

# ABOUT THE AUTHOR
## Phakamisa Ndzamela

Image: Freddy Mavundla

*Phakamisa Ndzamela is an award-winning former business journalist for Thomson Reuters, Business Day, Financial Mail and Moneyweb.*

*He holds a BA in Politics, International Relations and BA Honours in Journalism from the University of the Witwatersrand.*

Ndzamela invests a portion of his free time in the archives, weaving through the dusty boxes, in search of untold business stories. His goal is to use research to immortalise the lives of those whose stories remain hidden.

# ACKNOWLEDGEMENTS

## *The founders of African Bank, Long Live to your undying spirit!!!*

This book project would not have been conceived without the vision of the entrepreneurs who set in motion the idea to create a bank for the people, by the people, serving the people.

I am indebted to the African Bank leadership led by the Chairman Thabo Dloti and the Chief Executive Officer, Kennedy Bungane (KGB), for empowering their team to commission this independently written narrative of African business *historia.* Over a decade ago, as a young writer, I was afforded the chance to imbibe wisdom at the wellspring of knowledge that Dloti and Bungane so generously offered. They taught me a lot about asset management, insurance, banking and corporate activity in general. Without your patience and lessons, I would have written less about business. This project is a result of your selflessness.

Sbu Kumalo, my brother, you are the future! Your innovative ways of building brand equity and lasting legacies are nothing short of extraordinary. My heartfelt thanks for making me part of this heritage creation process. Andile Khumalo, *Avtomat Kalashnikova (AK),* my leader – thank you profoundly for your unwavering support and your kind words. I sat with AK over a cup of coffee on Bree Street in Cape Town, and within an hour we had a book plan. Our handshake and the sincere look in our eyes were enough to seal the deal – no thick contracts needed. We built this on Trust, Respect, and Integrity!

Courtney Chapple offered unrelenting support, enabling me to travel and access loads of archived dusty boxes where our history remains hidden. Courtney, your efforts made my journey smoother than I could have imagined.

The teams at the National Library of South Africa in Cape Town, the UNISA Archives and the National Archives of South Africa in Pretoria, contributed immensely to the completion of the manuscript. They worked tirelessly to retrieve all the material I required. I am grateful for all your efforts and hospitality at the reading room.

This project owes its existence to a network of connections. Elders and friends provided essential leads in locating some people. Allan Edward Wentzel, the first General Manager of African Bank was generous to share some insights on the days leading up to the incorporation of African Bank. *I am grateful to Allan.*

Tat' Bongani "SB" Bodlani, a friend to my late father, gave some hints on where to look for certain people, including his guidance on the pattern of the older generation of entrepreneurs transitioning from operational retailers to landlords. Thanks *Gaba!*

RS Siyila of RS Siyila Attorneys, an uncle to me, unlocked a door that gave me access to a very powerful and untold story. Enkosi *Myirha!*

Mam' Linda Bosman and all the children of Tat' Amos Nzimeni Gadi, I extend my heartfelt gratitude for the time you set aside to immortalise your father's legacy. Duma Gqubule was kind enough to put in a word for me to talk to Dr Nokuzola and Luvuyo Peter Ntshona, the brilliant children of the great entrepreneur Constance Ntshona and activist Vuyisile Scrape Ntshona. Thank you so much Mhlekazi! Vuyo and Dr Zola, it is because of you that the story of Connie Ntshona will be told for generations to come. *Nkomoshe!*

AK provided me access to Khudu Pitje, the son of the cinema entrepreneur HM Pitje. Khudu was generous enough to open access for me to engage with Mam Vuyelwa Pitje. Her memory was impeccable and largely aligned to the archived records at my disposal. Enkosi Gogo Vuyelwa. *Kea leboga!!*

My brother, Mukoni Ratshitanga, I am grateful for your insights on Mme Sally Motlana and the evenings spent nursing Left and Right Bank Bordeaux refreshments . Ferial Haffajee, thank you so much for your constant support, opportunities and readiness to accommodate me. I must express my gratitude to Colin Bundy for his willingness to guide me on matters I did not have answers to.

Before completing the manuscript, I needed an editor with the adequate postgraduate qualifications to handle the primary researched work. Sis Viwe Tlaleane recommended Dr Bheki Mpofu as the ideal candidate. *Enkosi MaXaba!*

Ntate Makume Tlaleane. I see you Phoka. Thanks for everything. I am indebted.

Bra Bheki contributed immeasurably. He engaged the copy intellectually, making the necessary edits without taking the role of a ghost writer. Dr Mpofu offered enormous guidance on layout and design. His professionalism is admirable.

To the entire team at Brave Group, you were an integral part of the journey. Thank you for bringing this beautiful product to life.

Tembeka Ngcukaitobi and Wandile Sihlobo were the pillars of motivation, offering support when the going was tough. Chuma Ndzamela read parts of the manuscript and played the role of an enthusiastic supporter. My mother, Zoe Ndzamela, was the vigilant guardian of my wellbeing, always cautioning me about my lack of sleep.

Lastly, my profound gratitude goes to my wife, Matshema. She bore the brunt of my absence and frequent travels; I spent countless weekends away as a nomadic researcher. I am indebted to Matsh and our children, Noli and Vuli, for all the support.

Apologies to those who I forgot to mention.

Above all, I am immensely thankful to God for the boundless energy provided!

# Publisher Information

Published in South Africa by:

**Rockhopper Books**

Unit A Victory Park

Capricorn Business Park

Muizenberg

7945

**www.rockhopperbooks.co.za**

ISBN: 9 780796 151599

Copy Editor: Bheki Mpofu; Cover Design: Kirsten Pictor; Typesetting: Samantha Singh

**Additional photo research:** Phakamisa Ndzamela

**Cover artwork:** Brave Group

**Book design and layout:** Brave Group

"bietjie bietjie maak meer."

— AN Gadi

"Notwithstanding all the hazards that we face as African traders; we are not asking for charity. We want to stand on our own feet."

— Constance Ntshona

www.ingramcontent.com/pod-product-compliance
Lightning Source LLC
Chambersburg PA
CBHW051929190326
41458CB00026B/6451